All the time

DAILY DEVOTIONS FINDING FAITH IN THE EVERYDAY MOMENTS

Meredith Barnes

FAITH AND FORTITUDE PUBLISHING

FAITH AND FORTITUDE PUBLISHING

Los Angeles, California

Published by Faith and Fortitude Publishing

www.FrecklesandFortitude.com

ISBN: 978-1-7359056-0-0 paperback

ISBN: 978-1-7359056-1-7 ebook

Printed in the United States of America

To Ben, Campbell, Warren and Everett,
who I spend the most time with.

Contents

Forward

As a Hollywood writer and producer for 30 years, I learned "Time is money." It was an important lesson. But as a Christian I know Time is much more than that. My daughter Meredith Barnes knows that as well.

The Psalmist tells us Time is a gift: "Teach us to count our days that we may gain a wise heart." Einstein humorously tells us it's a scientific conundrum: "The only reason for Time is so that everything doesn't happen at once." And St. Peter tells us it's a spiritual mystery: "With the Lord one day is like a thousand years and a thousand years like one day."

Frederick Buechner advises us: "Listen to your life. See it for the fathomless mystery that it is. In the boredom and pain of it, no less than in the excitement and gladness...because in the last analysis all moments are key moments, and life itself is grace."

This sentiment seems to be the central theme of Meredith's book. She examines the moments of her life and sees that Time is grace. A mysterious gift we can use to create a spiritual rhythm to our lives; a rhythm in which we gain a wise heart and a calm center to face life when everything seems to happen at once. A rhythm that weaves all the moments of our lives into the heart of God and gives us the confidence to turn mysteries into adventures.

So, take a deep breath, get comfortable and start your adventure with Time.

David McFadzean
Co-Creator of the TV show Home Improvement.

Introduction

I started writing this book in the middle of a pandemic. Let's just stop and reread that first sentence. What? Such a strange concept. Anyway, there I was, quarantined in my house, with three children ages five, three and one, and there was no space or time for what I wanted. I wanted time to clean the house without anyone creating a mess immediately after I had straightened it up. I wanted quiet moments during which I could immerse myself in contemplative prayers. But I also was aware that somewhere deep under all the stress and worry of a family forced together with no escape (yes, a little dramatic) there was a gift. The gift of time. In the midst of worrying about my loss of time for myself, I was starting to see the time we were able to have together as a family.

Here's the thing about time: It's everywhere. I can't avoid it. I can't get it back. Time can feel like a gift and a curse. I've had a relationship with time for as long as I can remember. Time finds its way into everything I do. So, with that in mind, I wanted to take a deeper look at all time has to offer. How God uses time, how I use time, and how I can make better choices with my time.

I hope this book is an encouragement to you. I avoided sharing my writing for a long time. I was afraid of not being good enough. I worried someone had already written the words I wished to share—and perhaps even did a better job. I let my fear slow me down. I let self-doubt waste my time.

It took a severe loss of personal time to force me to see the abundance that time has to offer. And I would be remiss not to mention that it is truly a gift of abundance from God. His first gift to us was light. A light that allowed for time. My hope is you begin to see time and God through different eyes as you read this book. I want these words to meet you where you are right now.

When I wrote this book I had hoped that my relationship with time would change. I would be healed of all anxiety, frustration and fear. I would be more present and productive in my life. That didn't happen, not completely. The thing is, reading (or, in this case, writing) something doesn't change you. It is not likely you will finish this book and be healed of all the bad habits you have created in respect to time. Change isn't passive. It doesn't happen to you. You must do the work to encourage change in your life. I must do the work. My desire is that this book is a start to your own personal healing in your relationship with time. While I wrote it to myself first and foremost, I pray that it will speak to you just as deeply.

The Bible translation I use throughout *All the Time* is the English Standard Version. There are questions at the end of each devotion, and there is space for journaling. The questions can be treated as self-reflection or as an invitation for discussion with those around you. Whether you partake on this journey individually or in community, I pray you see fruitful growth in the time spent.

In the Beginning

In the Beginning

In the beginning God created the heavens and the earth. The earth was without form and void, and darkness was over the face of the deep. And the Spirit of God was hovering over the face of the waters.

Genesis 1:1–2

I F YOU ARE like me, the beginning of things is an exciting time. I love the start. The preparation. The blank sheet of paper. The endless opportunities in what lies ahead. The beginning is special because no mistakes have been made yet. But beginnings can become an idol to me. And that idol can paralyze my creativity. An idea is always at the center of the beginning. And sometimes that idea is so perfect in my mind that it starts to seem impossible for reality to meet my expectations. There are many times I have stalled at the beginning of something for fear of imperfection. I have procrastinated or simply abandoned perfectly good ideas because I wasn't sure of what the product would be. The beginning is the easiest time to give up, because I don't actually see it as giving up. If I stop before I start, no one will ever know. To have no one know I had an idea that might not be successful—doesn't that feel safer? The fear of failure and imperfection are the beginning's biggest adversaries.

In Genesis 1 we see the greatest beginning, the beginning of the universe. The beginning of everything. God had the ultimate idea. He thought of you. And you know what is the most empowering part of God's creation story? He knew it would be flawed. He knew there would be mistakes made by us humans along the way. Not small, insignificant mistakes—big, giant, brother-killing, flood-inducing, wife-stealing mistakes. Can you imagine starting with an idea, the most perfect idea ever, and knowing it would be flawed? That it would never be free of imperfection? God knew we would mess things up, and yet, that didn't stop him from moving forward.

Now, it's true, God had a plan for our mistakes. And not just any plan. He had Jesus, a Son who would perfectly enter our imperfect world and soak up all of our shortcomings. But just because we're absolved by grace, does not mean that on this earth, in this time, we are perfect. We're still flawed. We're God's flawed creation. And he made us anyway.

QUESTIONS

1. Are you excited or scared by beginnings?

2. Do you find you jump into something and then abandon it when things go awry? Or do you never start for fear of failure?

3. Do you believe God made you with intention?

4. How do some of the "big mistakes" of the Bible make you feel in respect to your mistakes?

5. What is something you've been putting off starting? Why?

6. What is something you've started and abandoned? Why?

Let There Be Light

---

*And God said, "Let there be light," and there was light. And God
saw that the light was good. And God separated the light from
the darkness. God called the light Day, and the darkness he called
Night. And there was evening and there was morning, the first day.*

Genesis 1:3–5

I'VE BEEN TO Alaska. I went in May one year when the days are
long and the nights are hard to find. It's amazing how quickly
I can get disoriented without the partnership of night and day.
There is a loss of place. And no matter how hard I tried to block
out the light, when it was time to go to bed, it was impossible to
make it feel like night. When I returned home and was welcomed
by the sweet relief of night, true darkness, I was given a glimpse of
the gift God designed for us.

God creates time. It's the first day of his big idea. He's at the
beginning, thinking about you, and he creates light, separates it
from the darkness, and gives you time in the form of day. If I'm
being really honest with myself, I think I go through most of my
life viewing time as the enemy. It is something to endure, count
down, manage, set alarms for, cram in. I never have enough of
it—or it goes too slowly. There's rarely a day when I have a purely
pleasant interaction with time. If I look at this closely, I realize I am
already complaining about the first step in God's big idea!

What if, instead, I looked at time as God's first gift to me? God created light in the form of day and then paired it with the darkness of night to give me the gift of time. I claim to be grateful for the time I have here on earth. But do I truly have a positive relationship with time?

Time is not our enemy—it is our gift. Time is the beginning of our story. Time grounds us and is designed to help us.

QUESTIONS

1. Do you see time as something you are working with or against?

2. How can you work toward treating time as a gift?

3. Are you selfish or generous with your time?

The Rhythm of Time

And there was evening and there was morning, the second day.

Genesis 1:8

And there was evening and there was morning, the third day.

Genesis 1:13

And there was evening and there was morning, the fourth day.

Genesis 1:19

And there was evening and there was morning, the fifth day.

Genesis 1:23

And there was evening and there was morning, the sixth day.

Genesis 1:31

E ACH DAY IS different. Some of you like the adventure a new day brings. Others (me included) prefer few surprises. Whether you are a person of routine or someone who seeks out new experiences each day, God understands.

I am drawn to routine, habit, schedule, consistency, whatever you want to call it. In my best moments I call it discipline. In my worst I call it controlling. As I read through Genesis, I notice that within the first six days of creation one thing stays consistent—there was evening and there was morning. Whether I want to look at the week of creation symbolically or literally, there was a lot happening in that first "week" of life. The world was literally changing. But I see that as much as things were changing, one thing stayed constant: time. Even in the drama of the beginning, there was a rhythm.

Evening, morning, evening, morning.

We all live within the rhythm of time. Some days I feel I am fighting the rhythm. I'm running late. I can't catch up. I'm behind the beat. It's easy to let time overwhelm me. After all, it stops for no one. In the moments when I get offbeat and feel behind schedule, I am challenged to stop and remember the purpose of time. It is God's reminder to me of his consistency in my life.

Evening, morning, evening, morning.

If I could start to see the rhythm and consistency of time as one of the most tangible examples of God's presence in my life, could I also see time as a comfort rather than something to struggle with? I like to arrive early for things, and I tend to get anxious when I'm late. Several years ago, I started practicing an activity whenever I perceived I was running late for an appointment. Rather than give in to my anxiety and attempt to rush, I would fight my instincts and slow down. I would ask myself this question after a few deep breaths: "What is going to happen if I am late?" Most often the answer to that question revealed my pride or the desire to be liked. No, I shouldn't be late to things. I'm not suggesting I throw caution to the wind and disrespect the time of those around me. I'm suggesting that in moments when I stop recognizing time as the first gift from God, an ever-present reminder of his consistency in my life, I stop, refocus, and allow myself to remember this is a gift. This is a rhythm offered to guide me.

Evening, morning, evening, morning.

QUESTIONS

1. Do you seek out routine in your day? Why or why not?

2. How do you feel if you are running late?

3. Do you see time as a reminder of God's presence?

God Takes Seven Days

But do not overlook this one fact, beloved, that with the Lord one day is as a thousand years, and a thousand years as one day.

2 Peter 3:8

WHY DID GOD take seven days to create the earth when he could have done it in the time it takes to snap your fingers? By taking seven days to create, he is creating time. We cannot exist outside of time. There is no journey without time. There is no story without the passing of time. No suspense, no relief. God knew our human existence needed a framework—a beginning, middle and end.

You know what really scares me? Eternity. When I was young, I would cry at night at the thought of heaven, living with no end, surrounded by angels and no change in life (or should I say afterlife?) circumstances. I don't actually want to live forever. I don't want to die, either, so figure that one out at a different time. But back to forever: I don't like it.

Eternity scares me because there is no framework. I need time in my day. I need to know when it's time to wake up, eat lunch, pick up kids from school. I need to know when to start the countdown to putting my kids to bed each night. I need time to orient my emotions and my actions.

I think God knew the absence of time would scare some of

us mortals. We need a before and after. We need a story. We need birthdays. We need to be able to visibly mark off time to have a sense of movement in our lives. We need time.

QUESTIONS

1. What do you think about God not needing time? Is that overwhelming? Comforting?

2. Do you think God took seven days to create the earth and its inhabitants? If not, why do you think the time frame of seven days was chosen in this passage?

3. How do you feel about eternity?

The Word Became Flesh

In the beginning was the Word, and the Word was with God, and the Word was God. He was in the beginning with God. All things were made through him, and without him was not any thing made that was made. In him was life, and the life was the light of men. The light shines in the darkness, and the darkness has not overcome it. … And the Word became flesh and dwelt among us, and we have seen his glory, glory as of the only Son from the Father, full of grace and truth.

John 1:1–5, 14

WITHOUT DIVING TOO heavily into theological ideas here, let's see Jesus for who he is. He is with God and he is God. So, in summary, Jesus is confusing. Maybe that's why John uses the imagery of calling Jesus the *Word*. I've always loved this passage. As a writer, I find it poetic. The imagery that is used speaks to my creative side. The Word becomes flesh. Here's why I find this passage exciting, beyond its romantic imagery: It's a reminder that there is power in what we say. What we say becomes what we do.

Most of our ideas stay just that—ideas stuck in our heads with no exit ramp. It feels safe to keep our thoughts private. There is no judgment. There is no one telling us they are bad ideas. But there is also no reward. How many ideas have you refused to put words to for fear of failure or judgment? If you are waiting to have the best idea before you put words to it, stop. God already did that with Jesus, the Word made flesh.

Speak up. There is a time to put words to your plans, ideas, and dreams. Could God think it and it happens? Sure. But this passage says God speaks it. Imagine how many ideas are stopped before they start because you don't put words to them. What would happen if you started seeing the power of your words in relation to action? If the Word could become flesh, there are no limits to what your words can accomplish.

QUESTIONS

1. What stops you from sharing your ideas with others?

2. Do you recognize the power of your words?

3. Do you see how words lead to actions?

Jesus Is the Beginning

Jesus said to them, "Truly, truly, I say to you, before Abraham was, I am."

John 8:58

DON'T MESS UP. *Don't mess up. Don't mess up.* For a long time, this has been the mantra that has unknowingly played in my head. I've got to be a good person. I've got to do it all right. I can't mess up. "Mess up" has meant a lot of different things to me throughout my life. Sometimes it has stood for sin. Sometimes it has stood for ambiguous life decisions that didn't follow a clear path. The problem is, of course, I mess up. I sin, I make bad choices, I make the wrong choices. For some of you this may seem like no big deal. We all mess up; it's fine. In the past I had a hard time understanding that.

How many times have you heard, "Jesus died on the cross for your sins"? Well, I've heard it a lot. And instead of hearing what that statement is truly saying, what I was hearing was, *Jesus died for you, so you'd better not mess up. You'd better be the best version of yourself. After all, you know Jesus, so you should let that be enough to make you a near-perfect person. Sure, maybe before you knew about him dying on the cross you could mess up, but now, now that you know him? You can't mess up.* Anyone else?

So, my pattern would be: Be a good person, try not to mess up, mess up, feel really bad, ask for forgiveness, and try not to mess up again. This pattern created a strange relationship between me and Jesus—he was the guy I was always trying to impress.

Then, one day I looked at the timeline and realized Jesus died a long time ago. Obvious, right? I know, but here's the thing. I wasn't always looking at it that way. The fear pattern of messing up I just described centered around an Old Testament way of thinking. I was trying so hard to stay within the lines, that I was missing out on a relationship with Jesus. I was offering my guilt in the same way the Jews of the Old Testament had offered up sacrifices for their mistakes.

In John 8 I see that Jesus has been around longer than anyone understood at the time. Jesus was at the beginning just waiting for his big immaculate conception entrance. Even at the beginning Jesus knew I would mess up. Jesus' sacrifice on the cross occurred before I was born, before I could sin. He died because he knew I couldn't be perfect. When I figured this out, it changed my relationship with my mistakes and with Jesus. I no longer walk around, worrying about messing up. I now live my life knowing I am loved. I am loved enough that God, knowing my sins before I even existed, sent his Son as a sacrifice. He did this to have a relationship with me, not so that I would tiptoe through life, constantly worried about messing up.

QUESTIONS

1. Are you worried about messing up?

2. How does the fear of messing up affect your relationship with Jesus?

3. What do you do when you make a mistake?

Rest

God Rests on the Seventh Day

Thus the heavens and the earth were finished, and all the host of them. And on the seventh day God finished his work that he had done, and he rested on the seventh day from all his work that he had done. So God blessed the seventh day and made it holy, because on it God rested from all his work that he had done in creation.

Genesis 2:1–3

I DON'T KNOW ABOUT you, but this passage feels a little repetitive to me. We get it: God rested. Why does it have to be said three times in a row, using almost exactly the same words each time? Then I start to think about trying to talk to my children. There are times when what I am saying to them is really interesting, like what's for dessert or how many games we can play. They usually are dialed into every word I speak when I'm delivering good news. Then there are times when I'm instructing them: *Make your bed, Brush your teeth, Don't hit your brother.* It seems to me that those are the times I am the most repetitive. *Pick up your toys, PICK UP your Toys, PICK UP YOUR TOYS.* No new news is being delivered; I'm simply not being listened to.

Do you ever tune out the Bible? Do you stop listening to God? I do. To be fair, I don't just do it with God. There are times when I am driving, and I'm so used to the route I am taking that I go on autopilot and only realize it halfway to the destination. If you are disturbed by this, don't worry. I am, too. I tune out the familiar. I tune out the unpleasant. Sometimes I refuse to listen, for no good reason at all. God knows this about me. God knew this about me before I was even formed. Remember? He had that big idea that he knew would have some bumps in the road (you, me and our sin) and that he would have to enlist Jesus to fix it later. God knew I was going to tune him out.

Sometimes when my kids tune me out, I actually let it slide. I often conduct a risk/reward analysis as I am parenting throughout the day. If I do *x* then *y* will happen. Sometimes I don't want the fight. Sometimes I back down from the tune-out. In this passage, God is not backing down. What he's doing is important, and he's demanding I pay attention, even if it's just to snap me out of my Bible-reading daze to say, *What in the world? Why did I just read the same sentence three times?* Here's why.

Rest is important. I react viscerally to this statement. I am both excellent and terrible at rest. How is that possible? Really, it makes no sense. There are certain times when I can absolutely let myself off the hook. And then there are others when I refuse to put down the work, no matter how many times you tell me to.

Let's talk about rest. There is physical rest, and then there is mental rest. Both are important, but demand very different things of me. As a mom to three boys, I always have something to do. The house is never clean enough, there is always one more load of laundry, and some kid inevitably needs attention. My mind is scrolling all day. I have a hard time shutting off my to-do list mentality. I struggle sitting next to a pile of anything—clothes, books, toys, clutter. In many ways, this is an excellent mindset for a mother. I am efficient and driven by compulsivity to keep an organized, well-run household. The problem is, it's hard to turn off. Being a stay-at-home mom, I rarely leave my job as mom. There is no daily commute to and from work. There is no leaving unfinished business at the office. My home is my office. So when it's time to rest, I'm still twitching at things to do. I need God to tell me ten times that it's time to rest. I need permission.

Rest is a hard sell. There is always the pressure to do more, be more, make more. Even as I read Genesis 1, it's easy to pay attention. God is creating! This is where the action is. This is momentum. This is the journey. Then I get to Genesis 2, and he rests. I don't think God was tired. I don't think God actually needs rest, but he does it. And he tells me about it three times in a row. He does all this for me. He sets down his power, giving me permission to stop.

Stop worrying about what's next. God rests so that we can, too.

QUESTIONS

1. Do you ever zone out? When and why?

2. Are you drawn more to rest or work?

3. What does rest mean for you?

Jesus Is Rest

"Come to me, all who labor and are heavy laden, and I will give you rest. Take my yoke upon you, and learn from me, for I am gentle and lowly in heart, and you will find rest for your souls. For my yoke is easy, and my burden is light."

Matthew 11:28–30

DO YOU EVER feel like you can't rest? That one day wouldn't actually be enough? That you can't afford to escape the work, even for a day? For some it's hard to stop working. We have something to prove to ourselves or to those around us. There is an internal race or scoreboard in our heads and if we take a break, we won't be able to catch back up. We simply can't afford to rest.

From the beginning Jesus has been present to remind me to rest. In the Old Testament God sets the Sabbath before me as a reminder to put down my burdens, my work and my worries. The seventh day is for rest. In the New Testament Jesus comes to tell me I can rest in him. Whether this applies to our personal or our professional lives, Jesus is calling us to rest in Matthew 11. He knows our fear. What if we rest and fall behind? What if we rest and lose control? What if we rest?

But Jesus doesn't just tell us to rest in this passage. There is a second part to his statement: *Take on my yoke.* He is not telling us to rest from all of life's distractions and obligations and then return to the same commitments on our time once we are done. He's telling us to permanently rest in him. Jesus isn't just a resting place one day of the week or twenty minutes a day during our quiet time. Jesus is our resting place all of the time. It's hard to imagine resting in Jesus continuously. How do we gain true rest in him?

Well, I think in this case our resting is not just physical, but spiritual. Before Jesus arrived on the scene, God's people were bogged down by the law. There was a lot to keep track of, and it seemed like people were having a hard time not only maintaining the law, but also agreeing on what the law meant and how it should be carried out. And by the way: I'm not judging the Jews. I'm a Pharisee at heart. I love a good rule, and I love doing what I'm supposed to be doing. God saw how tightly people were holding on to that law and realized they could not let go. They could not find true rest. They were always worried about doing it *right*.

Jesus restores rest to us. Sure, we have to work in this world. We have jobs, careers, children. But we don't have to let those responsibilities take over. We don't have to let our work become our idol. What we do matters, but it doesn't need to be the ultimate, all-consuming, be-all and end-all of our lives. When I truly embrace this passage, when I take on Jesus' yoke, when I rest in him, my accomplishments and failures lose their grip on my identity.

Most days, work is synonymous with mothering for me. And let's be honest, there are no perfect days in parenting. But, when I rest in Jesus, the failure does not define me. When I can realize a good or bad day does not change my salvation, I am free to rest. I know that in the midst of juggling three kids imperfectly my worth does not change. For some of you, you need to hear the converse: On the best day, when you are firing on all cylinders, your worth has not changed. If you are truly resting in Jesus, no matter how high or low you get, you are the same child of God, called to rest in his yoke. This does not mean what we do does not matter, simply that our output, what we do or produce doesn't own or define us.

QUESTIONS

1. What is your relationship with work?

2. Do you rest in Jesus? How does this look in your life?

3. Do you make time for rest?

4. How does a good day at your job affect you?

5. How does a bad day at your job affect you?

The Importance of Rest

---

*And he said to them, "Come away by yourselves to a
desolate place and rest a while." For many were coming
and going, and they had no leisure even to eat.*

Mark 6:31

*It is in vain that you rise up early and go late to rest, eating
the bread of anxious toil; for he gives to his beloved sleep.*

Psalm 127:2

WHEN WE WERE pregnant with our third child, my husband, Ben, had the idea of us getting away for a night. It had been a rough go for us as parents in the months prior. So I was all too happy to get whisked away for an evening without kids. We stayed at the hotel where we had spent our wedding night (six years prior). It was an escape filled with every parent of young children's dreams: uninterrupted conversations, TV in bed, and actual time to eat our meals without dodging dirty hands and spilled milk.

When we came home, nothing had changed. Our oldest still woke up the next morning before five. We still had the laundry and dirty dishes, but we were refreshed. We were reminded of the blessings around us, even amid challenges. We were thankful for my parents, who stepped in to love our children when we needed a break. The means to choose a night of escape in a lovely location. Children who missed us when we weren't there.

There is power in the recovery. So often I hear the message that I must work harder, be more dedicated, take fewer breaks. Success comes from hard work. Hard work is important, and it does yield results. Yet, hard work without rest often leads to burnout and loss of perspective.

There are times when I allow the pressure to "do more, rest less" overwhelm my actions. My body needs rest. And so does my spirit. The challenge for me becomes not only to create time to rest from physical activity, but also to rest my mind. It is a battle for me to give myself permission to not get it all done. To not feel guilty for creating physical and mental space absent of productivity that can be measured. But the gift of rest is fortification when I return to the demands in my life. The pressures of this world will never leave us, whether it be parenting children, clocking in at the office or taking care of our own parents as they age. The perspective we gain when we rest restores in us the ability to return to the task at hand, stronger than before.

QUESTIONS

1. Do you feel the pressure to work harder?

2. What is the thing in your life that is hard to break away from in order to find rest?

3. What happens when you do rest?

4. Have you ever experienced a time when you rested and subsequently felt stronger?

Rest in Who You Are Now

*Not that I have already obtained this or am already perfect, but
I press on to make it my own, because Christ Jesus has made
me his own. Brothers, I do not consider that I have made it
my own. But one thing I do: forgetting what lies behind and
straining forward to what lies ahead, I press on toward the
goal for the prize of the upward call of God in Christ Jesus. Let
those of us who are mature think this way, and if in anything
you think otherwise, God will reveal that also to you.*

Philippians 3:12–15

I DO THIS ALL the time: I compare myself to a past or future version of myself. I diminish where I am currently because I know there is a better version of me out there if I just look far enough forward or back. Sometimes it feels like if I am not in constant motion, I will be left behind or labeled as lazy or unmotivated. Just because I perceive that I was a better version of myself yesterday or will be a better version of myself tomorrow doesn't mean I can't enjoy who I am today.

When I start worrying about how I compare to the past or the future me, I stop inviting God into the moment. Any time I start to see myself through the lens of "less than," I stop accepting God's plan into my life. By ranking myself in comparison to what could be or what was I am diminishing who I am right now.

I've had a lot of different body shapes throughout my life. My body has had many chapters in health and appearance. At eight I was diagnosed with juvenile rheumatoid arthritis (JRA) and was confined to bed and given a medicine that made me sick to my stomach. I quickly became extremely thin. Then, as medicines changed but my mobility did not, I became overweight. That cycle continued throughout my life as I attempted to find the "right" exterior version of me

When I look back at pictures of myself throughout my life, I can see clear changes in my appearance from year to year. It is easy to be hard on myself when I look at some of these pictures. But those past me's were still me. They were on the journey. They were having good days and bad days. They were growing into present-day me. And while I believe in being healthy, sometimes the focus on my appearance robbed me of the joy each moment had to offer. It is good to have goals. It is good to work toward the best version of myself. But when the pursuit of *best* starts to create a negative internal dialogue, it becomes unhelpful.

Stop rushing to be a different version of yourself and remember to enjoy the version you are now. It doesn't mean you can't improve. It doesn't mean you will grow stagnant. The more you appreciate who you are now, the more you will like the person you are tomorrow.

QUESTIONS

1. Do you compare yourself to past or future versions of yourself?

2. What can you enjoy right now despite not being where you want to end up?

3. How can you rest in who you are today?

How Do You Practice Sabbath?

For thus said the Lord God, the Holy One of Israel, "In returning and rest you shall be saved; in quietness and in trust shall be your strength." But you were unwilling.

Isaiah 30:15

O N A RECENT Sunday I purposefully put only one thing on my to-do list. It was a long weekend for me. Ben was out of town on a golf trip. My three-year-old went down with a stomach bug. And the general chaos of life felt like a lot to handle. Sunday arrived, and I knew I needed to rest—mentally and physically. Dare I say a Sabbath was calling?

So I left just one item on my list to accomplish: time in the Word and in reflection. As the morning progressed, however, I found myself kicking into "mom" gear and doing all the things I usually did. I baked muffins, did the dishes, and started laundry. I even began a new sewing project. *What was I doing?* My work is my home. It is always around me. My children never stop needing me. The chores are never perfectly complete. The written list may have contained only one thing, but my mental list was an endless cycle scrolling in my head. I hit a wall in the afternoon and had to call it a day. By the end of the day, despite having only one item on my to-do list, I still felt the frustration of not getting more things done.

The hard truth is, I feel guilty when I'm *not doing*. I feel uncomfortable with the pile on my desk, the dishes in the sink, or the toys scattered around the house. The world will always be calling me to do more. As I fight to resist wanting to be everything, I must remember the truth God gave us with Sunday: It is good to rest.

QUESTIONS

1. Do you practice a Sabbath (day of rest)?

2. What does that look like for you?

3. If you could only do one thing on a day of rest, what would it be?

Time and Anxiety

In a Hurry?

*Desire without knowledge is not good, and whoever
makes haste with his feet misses his way.*

Proverbs 19:2

ANYONE ELSE OUT there in a hurry? Patience is not a strength of mine. Sometimes I think my children have increased my patience; other times it feels like they have reduced it. Both are probably true. What I have learned is that nothing is made better by hurrying toward or through life. Slowing down has allowed the sweet moments of my life to reveal themselves to me—moments I might have missed.

Full transparency: I'm getting ready to send this book off to an editor. I'm doing my final read-through, and much to my chagrin I've discovered a chunk of the book was not saved on my last edit. This means that I've had to rewrite a good portion of it. I'm so close to completing this, and I'm really excited. I'm in a hurry. When I opened up this document and found a large portion of text missing, I exclaimed out loud, "No, Lord! I have no more stories to tell!" And then I realized I was in a hurry. I've really enjoyed writing this book. Part of why I'm eager to send it off is because I fear I will never stop tweaking it. But I'm also just as eager to have the finished product in my hands—to have something to show for all the hours I've devoted to this task.

What if I stopped worrying about where I would end up? What if I stopped focusing on the happy ending? What if, instead of rushing to the destination, I simply rested in the moment?

I'm so quick to make the list and just want to get to the part where every item is checked off. Sometimes my urge to reach the end makes me miss the journey, the here and now. There's nothing wrong with looking forward, but when the horizon becomes more important than the ground beneath my feet and the people standing around me, I'm missing the best part.

QUESTIONS

1. Are you in a hurry?

2. What have you missed by being in a hurry?

3. How can you enjoy the journey as much as the destination?

Will I Be the First?

For I know the plans I have for you, declares the LORD, plans for welfare and not for evil, to give you a future and a hope. Then you will call upon me and come and pray to me, and I will hear you. You will seek me and find me, when you seek me with all your heart. I will be found by you, declares the Lord, and I will restore your fortunes and gather you from all the nations and all the places where I have driven you, declares the LORD, and I will bring you back to the place from which I sent you into exile.

Jeremiah 29:11–14

I CAN'T TELL YOU how many times I've worried about a good idea. I have a lot of them (yes, I'm making fun of myself). The truth is I've thwarted so many of my own ideas that I don't actually know how many of them were indeed good. One of the biggest impediments to my ideas is the question, "Will I be the first?" Is an idea even good if it has already been done? The thought that I might work hard to accomplish something, and then discover that someone else has done it before me, stops me in my tracks.

I have stopped myself from writing this book, or any other book for that matter, so many times for fear of it already having been done. What if I'm just one of many? These are relevant fears in a day and age where everything has been done. It is hard to get in at the beginning of a good idea. We are a society of saturated ideas. So what, then? Should I stop dreaming? Should the probability of being one of many stop me from moving forward? I hope not.

The encouragement I receive from this passage is not the promise of welfare. It is the promise of relationship with God. He doesn't care if I'm the first person to the big idea. That has no bearing on his plan for me. His plan for me is a relationship with him. Every choice I make is either bringing me closer to or further from that relationship. And once I put that into perspective, the worry about being first starts to dissipate.

QUESTIONS

1. Do you worry about being the first at anything?

2. Have you stopped pursuing any good ideas because of this?

3. Does this stop you from celebrating other people's successes?

4. How can freedom in relationship with God give you permission to pursue an idea and stop worrying about the outcome?

Am I Too Late?

But Saul, still breathing threats and murder against the disciples of the Lord, went to the high priest and asked him for letters to the synagogues at Damascus, so that if he found any belonging to the Way, men or women, he might bring them bound to Jerusalem. Now as he went on his way, he approached Damascus, and suddenly a light from heaven shone around him. And falling to the ground, he heard a voice saying to him, "Saul, Saul, why are you persecuting me?" And he said, "Who are you, Lord?" And he said, "I am Jesus, whom you are persecuting. But rise and enter the city, and you will be told what you are to do." … So Ananias departed and entered the house. And laying his hands on him he said, "Brother Saul, the Lord Jesus who appeared to you on the road by which you came has sent me so that you may regain your sight and be filled with the Holy Spirit." And immediately something like scales fell from his eyes, and he regained his sight. Then he rose and was baptized; and taking food, he was strengthened.

Acts 9:1–6, 17–19

I AM SCARED OF it being too late—too late to change, too late to start something new. It's easy to talk myself out of something by saying, "I am too old/it will take too long/that ship has sailed." Too many times in my life have I allowed time to stop me from moving forward. And then there are times I haven't. Times I have stopped worrying about *too late* and have chosen action.

When I graduated from college with a degree in theology, I had no clue what I was supposed to do next. I had only pursued a degree in that subject as they were the classes I enjoyed the most, so I kept taking more of them. My first jobs out of college were in the ad/sales department for the Anaheim Angels and costuming for an independent movie as well as several plays. I was at a job interview to work for the Mrs. Universe competition (I was just as confused as you are regarding this one) when the person interviewing me said, "You are too smart for this job. You should go back to school to become a doctor." No, he didn't just pick that profession out of the blue—I had told him about other careers that I had considered pipe dreams when he had asked.

I had two options when I left that interview. I could ignore his advice, telling myself it was too late to become a doctor. After all, the only science class I had taken as an undergrad was The Chemistry of Food—that was how much I didn't jive with science. Or I could take the chance and decide it wasn't too late to try. I was in my mid-twenties at the time, which now seems young to me. But as I was contemplating my next life step and watching friends establish themselves in the world, I felt overwhelmed at returning to years of schooling. It felt like a step back rather than a step forward. Approximately one year and biology, microbiology, chemistry, organic chemistry, and many other science classes later, I started applying to schools to become a physician assistant. And when I started graduate school, I was neither the youngest nor the oldest student there. There were other people there who had also decided it wasn't too late.

Why do I tell you this? Because you need to hear it's not too late. Saul, who after his conversion became Paul, hated Jesus and everyone who was on Team Jesus. It was his life's work to hunt down and persecute and kill the people who chose to embrace Jesus' message. I love the story in Acts 9 because not only does Paul have a complete about-face with his life's purpose, but it also shows I can change my mind. I doubt Paul was pondering whether he should become a disciple. But when the time arose and Jesus confronted Paul, his life was changed. He took a new name and presented himself to the world as a follower of Christ.

Paul didn't have to do that publicly. He could have met Jesus on the road, had the conversion experience, and then slinked away quietly, ashamed at the realization of what he had been doing. But he decided it wasn't too late to do the right thing. He was so transfixed by his newfound love for Christ that he risked scorn, embarrassment, alienation and rejection. He believed it wasn't too late.

I became a PA in the fall of 2008, and then in 2014 I left the field and claimed a new path as a stay-at-home mom after the birth of my first son. I tell you this to say: I'm still not done. I'm still wrestling with the question, "Is it too late?" Over the years, I've grown more comfortable with this question's presence in my life. Stop the worry. Stop the conditions you place on yourself limiting your ability to change. You can resolve to change whenever you choose.

QUESTIONS

1. Have you ever felt that it was too late for something?

2. Do you avoid change because it's "too late"?

3. What do you think you would have done if you were Paul?

Embrace the Mess

Do not be anxious about anything, but in everything by prayer and supplication with thanksgiving let your requests be made known to God. And the peace of God, which surpasses all understanding, will guard your hearts and your minds in Christ Jesus.

Philippians 4:6–7

THERE'S SOMETHING ABOUT the feeling of extreme chaos that can calm. To be in the eye of the storm. There is something about the absolute loss of a plan that creates opportunity. Sometimes I'm capable of seeing this. Sometimes I'm able to look into the mess and see the potential for peace. Other times I fight for that original plan until I end up beaten and bruised.

It's true what they say—every child you bring into your family increases the chaos. Three kids deep, and I can remember the moment when each of them first entered our family and the reality hit: What had we done? With our first son we had a hard learning curve. As parents know, you don't know what you don't know. And we didn't know anything about how to survive a newborn. When baby number two came home, I realized how much free time I had had with just one child. When baby number three entered the picture, I was less stressed about the perfect sleep schedule and more concerned with feeling human. No, it's not that bad, but it is chaotic.

In many ways the addition of our third child didn't feel as dramatic as the addition of the first two. We knew most of the things to expect (although somehow we still ended up in the ER two days into his life, and he's fine). But the messes become bigger and harder to contain and my time is even more limited.

As you will probably figure out by the end of this book, I'm a firstborn, type A, control-loving kinda gal who hides most of her crazy fairly well. But I also like to share my struggles in situations like these in an attempt to relate and give comfort to all of my fellow gals who know just how they want their house to look and which way the dishwasher should be loaded (back to front, of course).

Here's what kids have taught me: Life is messy. Some days it looks more organized than others. My job is to embrace the mess rather than resist it. What does that mean? It means giving myself grace when I don't get my original to-do list done. It means altering my goals. It means putting my children's needs ahead of my own. It means being willing to go off course to discover a different day than I had planned, and that may just be the day I'm supposed to have.

The mess is not here to make me anxious. The mess is here to turn me toward Jesus. The mess is here to remind me I need divine help beyond my own capabilities. The passage above doesn't say, "Don't be anxious and, by the way, figure out the solution to all your problems and never complain." It tells me where to look when I am bogged down by the mess—I must turn to God. And in doing so I am showing a willingness to trust God over myself. When I accept my limitations, and therefore the mess, I position myself to accept peace, even in the midst of chaos.

QUESTIONS

1. How do messes make you feel? What about chaos?

2. What do you do in times of stress or anxiety?

3. What is one practical way you can attempt to embrace the mess?

When the Plan Changes

The heart of man plans his way, but the LORD establishes his steps.

Proverbs 16:9

MAN, I LOVE to pout. I love to stew. I am so good at moping. And it's usually centered around something changing without my say. And then, after sufficient time of making sure it has been well documented I'm not happy with what's happening, I find a way to get on board. I almost always come around. I almost always recognize my moping has not stopped the change from occurring. And yet, time after time, I drag my feet in the face of change.

For a long time I excused this behavior. I explained that this was my process. This was how I was able to embrace change and get on board. But the truth is, the process stinks. It usually makes me look ridiculous and it causes strife with those around me. I'm not suggesting I can't grieve a change. But I am suggesting I do it with class and grace.

Ben and I visited San Francisco several years ago. When we started planning our trip, my one request was that we visit the Redwoods. On the day we planned to leave the city to visit the Redwoods, we rented a car, drove for over an hour, and arrived—only to find out we needed reservations to park when visiting the Redwoods. I wasn't happy.

Here's what resulted from our change in plans: We got creative. We decided to go to Golden Gate Park. It wasn't on our list of sights to visit, and we probably wouldn't have gone had we not had a morning open with a car. We were completely off schedule. In the midst of our change of plans, I remembered my favorite part of vacationing with Ben—we adventure well together.

But the truth remains: I am so good at acknowledging the *conceptual* need for the unexpected. But so bad at embracing the *actual* unexpected. I cannot sit here and tell you that all changes in plans are good or needed. But I can tell you that when I cannot see the good in the plan changing, I still have a choice. I can put my faith in my plans ... or put my faith in God and his eternal plan. The more I am able to focus on God's eternal plan for my salvation, the more the disappointments of this world lose their power over me.

Over the years I've started asking myself these questions when an unexpected change in plans occurs, to help me gain perspective: What is really bothering me about this change? Am I able to share this with someone I trust (most likely my husband or a trusted friend) without dumping on them or fighting with them? Can this lead to a constructive conversation? And most importantly: Am I trusting God and his plan in the midst of unforeseen change?

When rooted in the belief that God is establishing my steps, I loosen my grip on the plans I have made. The plans will change. Our plans in this world are transient. Let us see them as just that and rest in the eternal plan, the one that will never change.

QUESTIONS

1. How do you react to a change in plans?

2. How do you cope with change?

3. How can you use your eternal salvation to combat the anxiety that comes with change?

The Pursuit of Busy

Now as they went on their way, Jesus entered a village. And a woman named Martha welcomed him into her house. And she had a sister called Mary, who sat at the Lord's feet and listened to his teaching. But Martha was distracted with much serving. And she went up to him and said, "Lord, do you not care that my sister has left me to serve alone? Tell her then to help me." But the Lord answered her, "Martha, Martha, you are anxious and troubled about many things, but one thing is necessary. Mary has chosen the good portion, which will not be taken away from her."

Luke 10:38–42

I'M JUST SO *busy. How am I going to get it all done? There aren't enough hours in the day!* All these things I say to myself on a regular basis. Several weeks ago we were told to shelter at home in light of COVID-19. There are no longer school drop-offs. No play dates, story times, workout classes, idle Target trips. There has been a sudden stop to our sometimes overstuffed daily preoccupations. An unnerving quiet from the usual buzz of rushing from one thing to the next. My temptation right now is to continue to pursue busyness. Life as I've known it is vanishing at an alarming rate. And I'm finding busyness is a choice. Even with a blank slate, my mind moves quickly to maintaining a schedule.

Every time I read this passage, it takes me a minute to not be slightly irked by Jesus. After all, Martha is hard at work, serving those around her. She is getting things done in the kitchen. She sees a need and she is filling it. Martha is my kind of gal. I am Martha. While we are at it, I also understand Martha's frustration at Mary getting Jesus' undivided attention. What the heck? I want the credit! I want recognition for my busyness.

Jesus doesn't see it that way. He cuts Martha to the core, and me too. He sees my tendency to busy myself and he tells me to stop. The busyness is a distraction from Jesus. It stops me from being present in any given moment and invites anxiety into my day.

So here I am, in the middle of a pandemic, searching for busyness. Somewhere in this mess is a gift. It seems small and almost irreverent to acknowledge it—the gift of time. We are together as a family. Playing games. Going for walks. Reading books. The six little eyes looking up at me see this as one big adventure. This small gift. So, each day I attempt to set aside the pursuit of busyness and welcome the gift of time.

QUESTIONS

1. Do you identify more with Mary or Martha in this passage?

2. Do you pursue busyness?

3. What are some things you do simply to stay busy?

4. How does being busy make you feel?

5. Are you pursuing Jesus amid your busyness?

How We Use Our Time

Are You Selfish with Your Time?

Whatever you do, work heartily, as for the Lord and not for men.

Colossians 3:23

A
S AN INTROVERT, I guard my time. I mentally map out my days and weeks with the most prevalent concern being, "How much time am I getting for myself?" I am not the person who eagerly says yes when someone requests my time. As I have mentioned before, children require a lot of time and attention. As we have become savvier over the years, Ben and I have started to gift each other time.

Ben is an avid golfer (and good, I might brag—I mean, add). But the thing is, golf takes forever. Eighteen holes of golf, which is customary for one round, takes a minimum of four to five hours. You heard that right. As you can imagine, Ben's golfing and how long it takes has been the source of many disagreements over the course of our marriage.

It's taken seven years of our seven-year marriage for us to learn how to not fight about golf (clearly, we are still working on it). The fight is always centered around time: how long it takes, Ben not being home at the time he says he will be, me feeling I'm giving him this time for myself but not getting it in return, and both of us tallying up who is getting what time and the inequality that we feel from this.

Without a doubt, Ben and I are guilty of being time score-keepers. Over the years we have improved on this flaw. We have attempted to respect each other's time and to find space for both of us to get away. While in the past I have focused on tallying up Ben's hours versus my hours, I've learned no one wins when I keep a time scorecard.

In order for me to step closer to being generous with my time, I must release the feeling of time entitlement. I need to reorient my view of time, to see it as a gift from God. While I know, for my own best personal health I need time to myself, I also know it is good to be generous with my time, whether that be with Ben or anyone else.

Often, I want it to be all about me. I'm the center of my own universe. It's hard to truly look around and realize I'm one part of a greater picture. I think I want God to use me—until he asks me to sacrifice my time. In Colossians 3, the key takeaway is to do it for God, not anyone else. This becomes a clear indicator of how I should be spending my time. When I'm not checking in with God, it is easy to say yes or no to different demands on my time based on how I feel. Does it fit in my schedule? Do I want to do it? When I start seeing my actions as a call to serve God, I ask different questions. Will this serve those around me? Will this further the kingdom?

I know, it's hard to argue that Ben's golfing is furthering the kingdom. But it might be. Golf brings him a mental rejuvenation, allowing him to return to us, his family, a better husband and dad. The interactions he has on the course with other golfers may lead to spiritual development with men who might never step inside a church. (Please make sure to tell my husband I am defending his golf. It will go a long way in kiss-up points).

When I am selfish with my time, I am preventing God from using me to serve others. When I answer the call, I am simply telling God that my time is his to use.

QUESTIONS

1. Are you selfish with your time?

2. Are you guilty of being a time scorekeeper?

3. Do you spend your time based on what you want or what God wants?

4. Can you name a time when you did something you didn't want to do but felt it was what God wanted?

Are You Wise with Your Time?

Look carefully then how you walk, not as unwise but as wise, making the best use of the time, because the days are evil. Therefore do not be foolish, but understand what the will of the Lord is.

Ephesians 5:15–17

THE DANGER, WHEN discussing wisdom in respect to my time management, is the temptation to equate efficiency with wisdom. While I firmly believe in efficiency, the two concepts are not synonymous. I wear a Fitbit to track my steps. My goal is 10,000 steps a day. Yet, I still look for the closest parking spot at the grocery store. I'll ask my husband to get me water when I'm sitting on the couch and don't want to move. I'll opt for the Starbucks drive-through, even when I don't have a kid in the car. And I'll even occasionally enlist my three-year-old to run the odd errand throughout the day.

Walking into the gym one day from a particularly faraway spot (because there were no closer ones available), I was struck by my tendency to pick what is convenient. I live in a world of convenience. Time is a drug. I never have enough of it. I am racing to gain as much time as I can.

But what am I racing toward? I believe in using my time wisely, but I also have to battle constantly moving past moments. I don't want to take shortcuts at the expense of the experience. When I equate being wise with my time to being efficient with my time, I lose the opportunity to understand the will of the Lord.

And yet, simply slowing down and avoiding efficiency is not the answer, either. I have struggled with procrastination in my life. As I've mentioned before, I definitely gravitate toward a more buttoned up and organized personality, but have to admit I can procrastinate with the best of them. I've learned that if I don't tackle a task immediately, I tend not to do it at all.

So, where does this leave me? How do I achieve wisdom in respect to my time? I look to Ephesians 5. I slow down but continue to move. I look carefully at my days; I do not rush. I attempt to savor the current hour while also working to the best of my abilities to create a God-inspired future.

The first year of a baby's life is all the things: slow, fast, frustrating and amazing. What I've learned about these first twelve months is to attempt not to wish away the time. It's easy to long for full nights of sleep. It's tempting to put my head down and survive. And to some degree, it's necessary. But what happens at the end of the year is the baby has radically changed from the sleepy-eyed newborn to an on-the-move toddler with opinions despite a lack of words to reasonably convey them. And if I simply keep my head down focusing on the destination of a full night's sleep, I miss the depth of joy God offers in the first smile and deep baby giggles. I miss the miracle of a hand clap that expresses joy for a wordless one-year-old.

There is a lot to get done in my days. My task is to seek wisdom. Sometimes this means accepting slowing down; other times it may mean speeding up. When I place God at the center of my life, I see time as a gift to be spent wisely.

QUESTIONS

1. Do you tend to procrastinate or seek efficiency?

2. What does being wise with your time mean to you?

3. Are you wise with your time?

4. Do you know anyone who is really wise with their time?

Are You Aware of Your Time?

*Not that I am speaking of being in need, for I have
learned in whatever situation I am to be content.*

Philippians 4:11

M Y EYES TEND to lift up from the immediate and search
for what is next. When I was twenty-eight weeks
pregnant with my third child, I struggled with not
looking too far ahead. My mind would drift to the future: the
baby's arrival, reclaiming my body as my own, meeting this new
member of our family. But I also knew the struggles that would
lie ahead: the sleepless nights, the unknown balance of parenting
three young children. It's hard not to look ahead. It's hard not to
rush past moments that seem small or insignificant. I often strive
to reach the next moment of relief rather than seeing the potential
in each minute of my day.

There is beauty in the hope of what's to come. There is excitement in the dreaming. How can I both look forward to the *next*
and also bring awareness to the here and now? I like to look forward to things, big or small. I go through my day with lists of
things I look forward to: working out, getting coffee, quiet time,
folding laundry while watching a favorite TV show. There is something lovely about assigning excitement to small moments ahead.

There will always be something to look forward to if I can find beauty in the details. And in loving the details of each day, I am waiting well while still looking toward what's next with excitement. In order to fulfill the call to contentment in Philippians 4, I must be aware of my time. I cannot be idly moving through my day. Awareness of my time invites me to move with intention. Not to speed past, but to participate in its unfolding.

QUESTIONS

1. Are you aware of your time?

2. Are you content?

3. What are some small moments in your day you look forward to?

Do Expectations Drive How You Spend Your Time?

Do not be conformed to this world, but be transformed by the renewal of your mind, that by testing you may discern what is the will of God, what is good and acceptable and perfect.

Romans 12:2

Y MOM RECENTLY told me that I am peer independent, meaning I don't easily conform to what everyone else is doing. Instead, I have somewhat of an internal compass that leads me toward or away from different activities. She said that this gave her great comfort when I was in high school because she knew I wouldn't get caught up in going too far down a not-great path, simply because that's what everyone else was doing. I can see this in myself. As someone who didn't have a lot of friends in the younger years of my life, I had to learn how to entertain myself.

While I still maintain a healthy dose of independence, with the oversaturation of social media I've become more aware of what those around me are doing. As a parent, I am flooded with information: the perfect birthday party for someone's child, the most amazing educational craft for toddlers. Singles are watching other people's fantastic dating life or the party they opted out of, or worse, weren't invited to. There is always something I am missing out on, and it is hard to avoid knowing it and subsequently feeling let down. Despite the fact that a picture on social media is displaying a few seconds of someone's life, I often let it infiltrate my expectations of what my life should look like.

In Romans 12, Paul is telling you to not let the expectations around you change your purpose or your actions. Know your needs. They won't be the same as the needs of others and that's OK. Don't let the pressure of comparison drive your actions. Your talents are specific to you. When you spend time focusing on the talents of others around you and how your strengths don't add up, you are distracting yourself and wasting time from the purpose you were created for.

QUESTIONS

1. Do you compare your life to the lives of those around you?

2. Do you sense the expectations of others in your day?

3. How can you combat others' expectations of you?

4. How can you combat unrealistic expectations you have for yourself?

Are You Prepared?

Prepare your work outside; get everything ready for yourself in the field, and after that build your house.

Proverbs 24:27

THERE ARE FEW moments in life when winging it is a good idea (spoken like a true planner). OK fine, there are plenty of lovely spontaneous moments in my weeks where no preparation is necessary. But I'm not talking about those moments. I know preparation isn't usually considered sexy. It's hard to get really passionate when discussing the merits of groundwork. Nonetheless, I stand by the belief that there is beauty in the *before*.

There is a case to be made for preparedness. A great party needs someone to plan it. A successful vacation to the beach needs a bathing suit packed. Not studying for the big test rarely yields good results.

I am known for loving the season of preparation, whether it lasts for a day or a month. In the preparation, I can look forward to what comes next. Or I can walk into a stressful moment with the confidence that I have done the work. What if you didn't just survive the preparation because you knew it was a necessary evil? What if you savored the moments leading up to what comes next?

When I prepare well, I can see the beauty of what is to come. In Proverbs 24 I am told to prepare and then build. That seems like a no-brainer, but then why do I avoid preparation at other times? In an attempt to be more organized, I started making my sons' lunches for school the night before. Many parents out there have done this before me, and now that I'm writing it out, it feels like common sense. But I had at least one child in school for two years before this occurred to me. In those prior two years I wasn't always rushing to get out of the house on time, but it was just that much more work in the mornings. Eventually I changed my lunch preparation routine and discovered a more enjoyable morning with my kids.

Whenever I'm bogged down by the mundane actions of preparation, I try to pray. If the action I am doing is for someone else in my life, I pray for them. The simple task of giving the preparation a purpose beyond the immediate lifts my eyes up and away from myself. Preparation leaves more room for a Spirit-driven life. When I rush, I am more likely to lose my temper and less likely to give grace to those around me.

God calls me to prepare. My life is arguably one big preparation for eternity. When I treat the smaller moments of my days as opportunities to develop a discipline of preparation, I am showing respect to the time I have.

QUESTIONS

1. Are you usually prepared?

2. Where is one place in your life you could be more prepared?

3. How can you find beauty in your moments spent in preparation?

Can We Do It All?

For everything there is a season, and a time for every matter under heaven: a time to be born, and a time to die; a time to plant, and a time to pluck up what is planted; a time to kill, and a time to heal; a time to break down, and a time to build up; a time to weep, and a time to laugh; a time to mourn, and a time to dance; a time to cast away stones, and a time to gather stones together; a time to embrace, and a time to refrain from embracing; a time to seek, and a time to lose; a time to keep, and a time to cast away; a time to tear, and a time to sew; a time to keep silence, and a time to speak; a time to love, and a time to hate; a time for war, and a time for peace.

Ecclesiastes 3:1–8

I HAVEN'T SPOKEN TO one mom who has it all under control. The fear of not devoting enough attention to our children pervades both stay-at-home moms and working moms. The desire to have an identity beyond my children pulls at me. I want to be fully present to my children's needs while having a clean house, a vibrant social life, time for myself, time for my husband—I want it all.

This is not unique to motherhood. It is a human condition. There is a constant pressure to be more and have more. There is never enough time to get it all done. Yet, I keep trying. I look around and compare myself to those I believe have it all under control. And I lament the things I didn't get done in a day rather than see all that I have accomplished. I forget to celebrate simply being present.

No, I can't do it all. Humans weren't built that way. Something always falls through the cracks. It's not because I am not enough. It's not because I am not trying hard enough. It's because there is a time for everything, which means everything can't happen at the same time. There is a time for my children and a time for myself. There is a time for cleaning and a time for the mess. There is a time for work and a time for play.

If I were able to do it all, I would miss the importance of time. God didn't create time to remind me of my shortcomings. He gave me time so that I could celebrate, mourn, seek, love, keep, and cast away. There is freedom in my inability to do it all. When I accept that I can't get all of it done, I am able to stay in the moment a bit longer. This in turn releases me from the pressure of doing it all and allows me to accept the here and now.

QUESTIONS

1. Do you feel pressure to do it all? How is that working for you?

2. What if you only had time for one thing today, what would that be? How about two things? Five things?

3. How can you release yourself from the pressure to do it all?

Time Brings Change

The Repetition of Time

---

*Again, for the second time, he went away and prayed, "My
Father, if this cannot pass unless I drink it, your will be
done." And again he came and found them sleeping, for their
eyes were heavy. So, leaving them again, he went away and
prayed for the third time, saying the same words again.*

Matthew 26:42–44

GOD SPEAKS TO me in repetition. Whenever I start hearing
the same concept or phrase being repeated in my life,
I start to take notice (see "God Rests on the Seventh
Day"). Oftentimes there is a lesson or change coming my way and
I know to prepare for what God has in store for me.

In Matthew 26, Jesus is in a cycle of repetition with those
around him. He is instructing the disciples to stay alert with him
in these last few hours of the night. He is coming to God, pleading
for a pardon. Each time Jesus comes back from prayer, he finds
the same thing: sleeping friends. And to make things worse, God
doesn't seem to have changed his mind, either.

Repetition might come in the form of running into the same
person several days in a row or having different people in my
life bring up the same subject matter to me without knowing it.
Sometimes, when I see these repeated themes, I get excited for
what's ahead. I love feeling God's interaction in my life. I take

comfort in knowing that it's not just me going from choice to choice. And if it's God ordained, it's got to be good, right? Well, no. Not really.

I've had many repeated signs appear in my life that were disappointing or even heartbreaking. Shortly before I met Ben, I dated a guy who, again and again, showed me he was not capable of loving me. I resisted these clear repetitions in his behavior. I was scared of being single and having to start the dating process again at thirty years old. Sometimes the repetition in life is just plain mundane. Dishes needing washing. Children asking the same question ten times a day. Laundry (which seems to be a big part of my life given all my references to it in this book) on constant repeat. Clocking in at an uninspiring job.

So, what do I take away from Matthew 26? What do I take away from the repetition in my life? It's OK to come to God repeatedly in seasons in which I feel stuck. Jesus is fully human and fully God. Don't ask me to dissect his DNA any further than that. What I can tell you is Jesus knows without a doubt he is going to do what he is praying to God to take away. The crucifixion is happening. Just as God resting on the seventh day is for my benefit, not his, Jesus praying three times to God is done to give me permission to do the same. To encourage me not to give up on crying out, even if it's my tenth time doing so.

Whether God is speaking to you through repetition, preparing you for the change ahead, or you are crying out to God about the same thing as yesterday or last year, don't miss what is waiting up ahead by avoiding repetition in your life. Pay attention to what others are saying to you or what you are saying to God or the people in your life. Being aware of the repeated concepts around you allows you to prepare for God's actions in your life.

QUESTIONS

1. What is God repeatedly telling you, or what are you repeatedly telling God?

2. Are you drawn toward or away from repetition?

3. Is there a way to see the mundane repetition of our lives as somehow sacred—a calling from God?

4. Can there be something ordained in the ordinary?

The Promise of a Fresh Start

We were buried therefore with him by baptism into death,
in order that, just as Christ was raised from the dead by the
glory of the Father, we too might walk in newness of life.

Romans 6:4

I LOVE A GOOD, fresh start. When done well, it can be just the morale boost I am looking for. When done halfheartedly, it can drag me down with guilt. I seem to assign this concept of a fresh start to specific times, mornings, months, years and ... Mondays. Raise your hand if you've ever planned to start something on a Monday. Now keep your hand up if you've fallen off the wagon before Tuesday has come around.

In the New Testament God is offering us a fresh start. Clearly, we humans are desperate for a better way, a new covenant. Enter Jesus. Crucified, buried, resurrected, and ascended. Quite the show-off, that Jesus. And then there's that word—*baptism*. In the New Testament baptism is a sign of accepting Christ into your life. Depending on where you go to church, talking about baptism can be tricky.

In truth, I've been baptized twice. Growing up in the Episcopal church, I was baptized as an infant. Later in life I became involved in a church that requested I be baptized as an adult in order to lead a Bible study. So I did it. Leading up to my second baptism I felt sort of silly. I've been a Christian my entire life, and while some seasons have been better than others, I've never doubted God or Jesus in my life. On the day of my second baptism, I showed up to Lake Michigan at sunrise with a large group from my church. Friends of mine came to support me. I walked into the water fulfilling an obligation, and I walked out with a new beginning. I'm not suggesting baptism every few years of life, but it's worth stating it's never too late for a fresh start.

Whether it's Monday or any other day. Whether it's the first hour of the day or the last. Change is in your power to create at any time, any place. Maybe your personality is well-suited for starting anew. Or maybe you are the person who is overwhelmed by the list you have created for yourself—the things you have told yourself you can do better.

Start small. Check one thing off your list at a time. Give yourself grace to miss an opportunity without it meaning you will not take another one. We are imperfect creatures working toward a perfect goal that will never be realized here on earth. But don't let that stop you from trying. Let this be the time for progress, no matter when you start.

QUESTIONS

1. How do you feel about fresh starts?

2. Do you tend to assign them to a certain time of the day, week or month?

3. Have you been baptized? If so, how old were you?

4. What does baptism mean to you?

What We Can't Imagine

*Now to him who is able to do far more abundantly than
all we ask or think, according to the power at work within
us, to him be the glory in the church and in Christ Jesus
throughout all generations, forever and ever. Amen.*

Ephesians 3:20–21

Y OU WOULD THINK that after having permed bangs in the second grade, things could only get better, right? Unfortunately for me, not true. We moved to California right before I started the second grade. I'm not sure the permed bangs helped me make many friends—to be clear ONLY my bangs were permed, the rest of my hair remained untouched and straight. Then, the summer leading into third grade, we moved just far enough over in our neighborhood that I had to switch schools. Nope, that was not the worst part, either. Somewhere at the start of third grade I got sick. Really, really sick. For most of third through fifth grade I was stuck in bed and homeschooled. As mentioned before, I was eventually diagnosed with juvenile rheumatoid arthritis. The main symptoms, at the time, being pain and joint destruction.

While no one could say what had caused it, they also couldn't say how long it would last. It could be forever, or it could go away once I grew up. It didn't go away and there were different stages and consequences of that. The main problem was, I was different. I couldn't walk well. I didn't play like other kids. I mostly kept to myself and read—a lot.

Why share this? Well, this morning, while running three miles, which I do at least four times a week these days, I had one of those moments of clarity when a simple truth hits me right in the face. In those moments, I can't help but be thankful, and perhaps a little introspective. If God himself had come down to eight-year-old Meredith and told me I would one day run for fun (yes, fun!) I would have said, "You've got it wrong," the way we often do with many of his promises. It didn't happen right away. There was lots of emotional and physical pain between eight and thirty-eight. But it did happen. So, as I was running this morning, I took inventory of what was really at play. I was moving and none of my joints were in pain. I was living my past self's unimaginable dream.

Where are you today? What is your unimaginable dream? What is the situation that you feel stuck in and think you will never move past? Don't give up on pursuing change. It may be subtle and take a long period of time. It may not look how you think it should look. But time does bring change. There are permanent scars from my RA. Some of my joints are still, and always will be, a mess. There are days it does hurt when I attempt to run. But here's where you come in. You have to make a choice. You have to choose to not let your limitations define your limits. You have to push yourself out of the misery, the fear of failure, the pain. The fear of, "This is as good as it will get." Because it can get better. It will get better if you don't settle for where you are today. Allow God to surprise you with what "better" can be. Not everyone will be healed. Not everyone will be free of grief. But when you invite God on the journey, you are likely to be amazed at the path he paves for you.

Don't forget to celebrate all of your successes. Sometimes you need to look back to where you've been in order see how far you have come. It would be easy for me to look at the runner who just passed me, pushing a baby jogger with a dog in tow and think that I'm less than because I'm not as fast as she is. Or I can celebrate where I am *and* celebrate that she is on her own path to success. My pace, my distance, my success is not diminished by other people's successes and does not trump anyone else's progress. It simply marks how far I've come. How far will you go?

QUESTIONS

1. What might be your unimaginable dream?

2. Have you had something that seemed out of reach come within your grasp?

3. How did that feel?

4. Do you believe God's power is at work within you?

Just Change Today

And as he was setting out on his journey, a man ran up and knelt before him and asked him, "Good Teacher, what must I do to inherit eternal life?" … And Jesus, looking at him, loved him, and said to him: "You lack one thing: go, sell all that you have and give to the poor, and you will have treasure in heaven; and come, follow me." Disheartened by the saying, he went away sorrowful, for he had great possessions. And Jesus looked around and said to his disciples, "How difficult it will be for those who have wealth to enter the kingdom of God!"

Mark 10:17, 21–24

SOME OF YOU out there find no difficulty in selling all your possessions and following Jesus. We call you the kiss-ups. OK fine, we call you the people who unquestioningly get it. I'm not that person. When Jesus says to kick your family to the curb, skip burying your parents and follow him, I'm not all in. I'm tentative. I'm fearful, because as much as I want and work toward a closer relationship with Jesus daily, I can't see him, smell him, touch him—and I really like my family (most days). It's hard to let go. It's hard to commit to upending my life for something I can't see.

What are some common obstacles to seeking change? Comfort in how things are now? The unknown of what it will be like after I change? Selfishness? When I look at Mark 10, I recognize this man is facing an overwhelming change. It's not only a change in physically giving up the comfort of his current life; it's also a change in his status to those around him. It's a life altering change. And change is hard.

I gave up meat five years ago. As a burger-loving, steak-eating girl living in Chicago, it seemed daunting to give up such a big food group. After thinking about it for quite a while and reading up on the benefits of a meat-free diet, I decided to give it a try when I was pregnant with my second child. I can now honestly say I don't miss it. When I first tried a vegetarian diet, I told myself this would not be for forever and that after an initial fast from meat for a few months, I would incorporate it back into my diet sparingly. Yet I haven't. I haven't wanted to.

I've recently decided to do a trial without dairy, for health-related reasons, and I love cheese. It's made me think about change. When I decided to give up meat, if I had told myself, *You will never have another burger*, the change would have seemed insurmountable. But the fact that I gave myself the choice—the fact that I said, *Let's just try this and see what happens*—gave me the freedom to try something without the guilt of failure or the fear of permanent loss.

Money and meat might not be in the same category when picking things to change in my life. And making a change for eternity with Christ is also likely to be categorized differently than making a change that has no eternal consequences. But the fact remains, I resist change. I give power to the fear behind making a change. I allow comfort in what I know to be more powerful in my life than the hope of what could be.

What if you only took it one day at a time? Would you act differently? Would you try more and put off less? Give it a try. Without worrying about tomorrow, make a change for today.

QUESTIONS

1. What change are you avoiding? What seems too big to try?

2. Would you find it easier to make a big change for yourself or for Jesus?

3. Are you holding onto anything too tightly?

To Embrace Change

Every good gift and every perfect gift is from above,
coming down from the Father of lights, with whom
there is no variation or shadow due to change.

James 1:17

T IME DOESN'T STOP. It keeps ticking by, no matter how hard I try to manipulate it. I cannot travel back or rush forward. Time simply is. And with each minute that passes, there is an opportunity for change to occur. Time literally is a quantifiable metric by which I can watch the world change. As someone who doesn't like change, I've recognized that this immediately puts me at odds with time. I'm a person of routine. My days tend to have some sort of pattern to them. And while I can try to create the best schedule, it will eventually have to change. Whether that's due to a sick kid staying home from school or a pandemic shutting down the world, time will bring change.

I will never have a peaceful relationship with time until I can start to work on my relationship with change. They come as a package deal. All vacations come to an end. Kids grow up. The seasons change. How do I evolve in my relationship to these two entities? I look to the Father of lights. Can you imagine no variation? I've just said everything is changing. God is the creator of time, and as its originator, he is above it. He is not subject to time. What this means is, he does not change. In the midst of whatever is happening in your life right now, God is.

When I look to the first part of this verse in the context of a constant God, never changing and always bringing me gifts, I start to look at change as an opportunity. How can I best prepare for the gifts God gives? I seek out opportunities for change. I seek out ways to embrace time. Something as simple as changing the order or way I do something may seem minor at the time, but might prepare me for the next gift of change. This is not to say I should create unnecessary, additional change for myself. But rather take an honest look at my routines, to discover areas where I have become so comfortable that I'm missing out on developing adaptability in my life or the discovery of a different way.

As I've stated before, I like to run. In my neighborhood I have a three-mile loop that I set out on each time I start a run. I always come out of my driveway, run down my street, and immediately turn right up a large hill to start my route. The other day as I laced up my shoes, I decided to turn left. I know, it seems silly. But this small change was evident to me immediately. My body had gotten used to the usual route. My eyes had become used to focusing on the same sights each time I ran. I discovered I had been running on automatic. When I did the loop backward, turning left and working my way in reverse around the same path, it was different. I saw things I had never noticed before. I had a new awareness for my surroundings. My body reacted differently to each step. And I discovered a new beauty in making this one small change.

I recognize that some of you are less tied to routine. Or are you? What do you reach for every morning when you wake? Do you need your morning coffee? Can you find times in your day that you also submit to autopilot? While routine is not the enemy, I can attempt to open my arms to change and practice accepting change in my life. In doing so I may see beauty that I am walking past without even noticing, due to routine.

QUESTIONS

1. Do you see God as constant and above time? How does that make you feel?

2. Which one habit could you change? How does it feel to change one habit?

3. Do you see change as a gift from God?

4. What is one change you didn't seek out that ended up being a gift to you?

The Power of Time

Are You a Victim of Time?

And the king said, "Bring me a sword." So a sword was brought
before the king. And the king said, "Divide the living child
in two, and give half to the one and half to the other." Then
the woman whose son was alive said to the king, because her
heart yearned for her son, "Oh my lord, give her the living
child, and by no means put him to death." But the other
said, "He shall be neither mine nor yours; divide him."

1 Kings 3:24–26

WOW. THIS PASSAGE freaks me out. I remember reading this story in 1 Kings as a child and being amazed at the prospect of Solomon cutting a baby in half; but now, as a mother, the grief I feel for both women is heavy. Talk about two women who are victims; this is it. One mother has slept so deeply that she inadvertently smothered her baby who was sleeping in bed with her. The other mother wakes to a lifeless baby who is not hers and has no idea where her baby is. In both situations the heartache and desperation are thick. I can't think of a worse setting. These mothers must *feel* like victims—one to a terrible accident, the other to a grieving mother who makes a deceitful decision.

When you are a victim or perceive yourself to be, your true colors often come out. How are you spending your time? You may go through your day feeling you are a victim of the minutes ticking by. That there are few choices you can actually make. You are stuck in a rut, doing the same old thing day in and day out.

Ben and I have been through many seasons when we have battled sleep with our children. I suppose it comes with the territory of parenting. In one particularly hard season, my oldest son woke up consistently before five each morning. On one of these mornings, I still hadn't recovered from the battle we had had the night before while attempting to get him into bed. I was wounded, tired, and out of patience. The only thing I knew for certain was that I was a ticking time bomb. Rather than fight for the next several hours about going back to bed, I made a choice. We went for a drive. We ended up in Malibu. If I'm going to be tortured in the early morning, at least I can do it in a glamorous location. And at any other time of day, it's impossible to get to Malibu from Pasadena in a reasonable amount of time.

I pulled over along the ocean, unbuckled my seat belt, and slid into the passenger seat. I reached back, unbuckled my son, and brought him up front with me. We sat there, listening to the same worship song on repeat, and I cried. I cried for my anger at a four-year-old. I cried for my feelings of inadequacy as a parent. I cried for the undeserved grace covering me, even as I fought with my child over sleep.

There are so many hard moments, ugly moments, moments to feel trapped in. As we sat there, parked on the side of the road, watching the transition from night to morning—me in tears, my son not quite understanding the complex emotions of his mother—I took a picture of the sunrise to remind me that I can always choose to find beauty, even in the midst of despair.

Every minute I have a choice. I have options regarding my attitude, my attention and my actions. And by choosing one path, I am also actively not choosing another. Sometimes that means sacrifice. Sometimes that means bringing awareness to my actions.

I have more power than I think. The power to choose positivity. The power to choose to encourage others. The power to be willing to learn. Make the choice today to reject being a victim to time. Even if it just means watching the sunrise with a sleepless child.

QUESTIONS

1. Do you feel like a victim to your day?

2. Are you spending your minutes aware of your power of choice?

3. Are you letting your circumstances drive your momentum?

The Strength to Endure

*Not only that, but we rejoice in our sufferings knowing that
suffering produces endurance and endurance produces character,
and character produces hope, and hope does not put us to shame,
because God's love has been poured into our hearts through the
Holy Spirit who has been given to us. For while we were still
weak, at the right time Christ died for the ungodly. For one will
scarcely die for a righteous person—though perhaps for a good
person one would dare even to die—but God shows his love
for us in that while we were still sinners, Christ died for us.*

Romans 5:3–8

I

T's TRICKY TO talk about suffering. Suffering is personal.
Often when talking to someone about a hard season they
are going through, they will eventually attempt to diminish
their suffering by acknowledging that someone out there has
it worse than they do. We tend to feel the need to qualify our
suffering. Suffering becomes something we have to earn the right
to talk about. While it is good to have awareness of other people's
circumstances, there is a missed opportunity in sweeping our own
suffering under the rug.

God gives me suffering as a gift. I can say this because suffering
is not the end of the story. I see God's redemption in suffering most
clearly on the cross. The cross where Jesus suffered and died for

sins not his own. But that isn't the end of that story—he was raised again. His suffering produces hope for me. And the hope is shown in his resurrection and ascension. But that's God, right? Of course his suffering produces hope. How can my suffering do the same?

I have a choice every time I encounter suffering in my life. A choice to become bitter or to become better. In today's world it is easy to simplify my daily encounters into a category of purely good or a category of purely bad. Got the job I want—good. Boyfriend broke up with me—bad. But what if that's not how God sees it? What if what I consider "bad" actually is good to God? What if every moment in my life is an opportunity to build character? When I suffer, I have an opportunity to turn to something for comfort—food, alcohol, money, TV and the list goes on. Turning to something other than God in my suffering will likely produce hopelessness, as these comforts can only ever offer a temporary relief. But when I turn toward God, I can see that suffering here on earth is not "bad" in his eyes. It's an opportunity to bring me closer to God. And if I truly believe in a life after this one, in heaven, with our Creator, I can see that suffering is not the end of the story.

How do I find hope in a situation of suffering? When I had two miscarriages back to back a couple of years ago, I already knew what suffering was like. I had endured affliction before. And so, even amid loss, I clung to hope: The hope that I would make it out the other side. The hope that God wouldn't leave me in my pain. The hope that when suffering is placed in my path, it is a gift from God, an opportunity to be refined. We all have suffering in our life. We all have the list of grievances that we carry with us. What we do with that suffering is what gives us the opportunity to develop character. If we can remove ourselves from the good/bad view of life here on earth and see it as an opportunity to grow, we can continue to cling to hope, even in our pain.

QUESTIONS

1. Have you experienced suffering in your life? If so, how has your suffering changed you?

2. Do you have hope in the midst of your suffering?

3. Do you tend to compare your suffering to the suffering of those around you?

4. How can you support someone you know who is currently suffering?

Changing Your Mind

*Trust in the LORD with all your heart, and do not lean on
your own understanding. In all your ways acknowledge
him, and he will make straight your paths.*

Proverbs 3:5–6

As I MENTIONED earlier, when I decided I wanted to go into
medicine, I had taken only one science class in undergrad. I
hated science. It wasn't my talent. Even still, I went back to
school and took the science classes I had avoided in college. When I
was accepted into graduate school to become a physician assistant,
I was admittedly surprised. I didn't have the same experience as
others in the program. I felt like a fraud for most of my time in
school. I was surrounded by really smart people. I had to work
twice as hard as almost everyone there. But I did it. I graduated
and got a job. And then years later, when I had my first son, I quit.
This made people uncomfortable.

I have had several women approach me about making big
changes in their lives. It seems scary. It seems overwhelming.
Sometimes it seems risky. All of those things are true. But the thing
that usually stops me in my tracks from making a big change in my
life is worry about what others will think.

When I tell people that I stay at home with my children, they
always want to know if I'll go back to being a PA. I usually say no.

It's the truth (as far as I know, but I can't see into the future after all). Medicine served me well. I can clearly see God's plan in the path I have taken. But medicine is part of my story. It is not my entire story.

What I've learned since leaving my career in medicine is that I have to be OK with other people's discomfort. If I am making the right choice for me, it's OK that others don't like or understand it. Changing my mind is allowed, even when it looks to others like I have wasted my time. This does not mean I am abandoning wise counsel. But it does mean a stranger's or acquaintance's probing questions and expectations do not define what is right for my life. There have been many times in my life when my path has felt crooked, weaving from one direction to the next. I have tried out a lot of careers. But what has felt winding to me has always been straight to God. Changing your mind in the direction you want to head, personally or professionally, doesn't mean the time you've spent is wasted. Moving closer to your purpose isn't a setback.

QUESTIONS

1. Is there a change you want to make but haven't yet because you are worried about what others will think?

2. Why are you letting this stop you?

3. Do you turn to God before you make big decisions?

4. Do you think your path has been straight or crooked?

5. Are you on God's path for you right now or on your own?

When Should Becomes Want

For the moment all discipline seems painful rather than pleasant, but later it yields the peaceful fruit of righteousness to those who have been trained by it.

Hebrews 12:11

A
s you know, I didn't play sports or do much in the way of physical activity as a child. I didn't have a sense of connection with or control over my body. It took me a long time to develop a relationship with my exterior that allowed me to see the results of taking care of it.

My first friend in college was Mary. I met Mary at orientation freshman year. She was a spitfire encased in an athletic five-foot-three frame. Mary was someone with passions, one of them being athletics, having been an avid soccer player in high school. Mary introduced me to the world of exercise. I had been vaguely aware that people played sports and worked out, but for the first time I could see into someone's daily activities and learn from what they did. Mary went to the gym every day. And so, to be like Mary, I started going to the gym too.

At first, I walked on the treadmill. Then gradually, I started running: a half mile, a mile, and slowly building up from there. I didn't like it. I wasn't good at it. I didn't even really know what I was doing. Most days I didn't look forward to working out; but

I did it because that was what Mary did. I would look at people leaving the gym and be envious that their workout was completed for the day. Yet I continued to show up, running shoes laced, ready to sweat.

When talking about this transition, I want to make something very clear: It didn't happen for a long time. I don't even know when exactly it did happen. My road to health has been just that—a road, a journey. There has been no quick fix. It has been small changes and sticking with something over time. And then, one day, the thing I had been making myself do became something I was thankful I got to do. Now, twenty years later, my mindset has changed. I look forward to working out. I am no longer jealous of the people leaving the gym. I am thankful to be able to move my body.

Should is a discipline. It is a grind. And somewhere along the way some of the things I should do have become things I want to do. But that doesn't make it easy. It's still not always a simple choice to get up and run, to eat the green foods instead of all the carbs. The trick is challenging my wants. Their motives, their truths and their lies.

There have been few times in my life when I've regretted being a disciplined person. In the early stages of creating a new discipline, I struggle to do the thing I should do, but gradually it becomes less difficult. Often, I even end up enjoying it. Discipline has helped me learn the difference between what I should do and what I want to do. *Should* has taken me on a journey that has changed me.

When I am attempting to be disciplined, oftentimes my wants are not aligned with each other. I want to lose five pounds, but I also want to eat a bottomless bowl of peanut M&M's. Still, not all wants are bad. When I attempt to discern the merit of my wants, I look to Hebrews 12. What will I want later? Right now I want comfort, but later I will want the result. If I can discern between

the wants of now versus the wants of later, I am more apt to employ the discipline of pursuing what I should do.

Questions

1. What do you do because you should?

2. What do you do because you want to?

3. When have they aligned?

4. When have they not aligned?

Your Choices Matter

---

*But Ruth said, "Do not urge me to leave you or to return
from following you. For where you go I will go, and where you
lodge I will lodge. Your people shall be my people, and your
God my God. Where you die I will die, and there will I be
buried. May the LORD do so to me and more also if anything
but death parts me from you." And when Naomi saw that
she was determined to go with her, she said no more.*

Ruth 1:16–18

M Y THREE-YEAR-OLD HAS started repeating the phrase, "I
go where you go, Mom." Sounds cute, right? Except
sometimes I'm going to get away. Sometimes I'm going
to the bathroom. Sometimes I'm not going anywhere. There is an
unconditional commitment I'm receiving from my son when he
says this. Despite not always wanting this dedication, whenever he
says this phrase, it brings me to Ruth.

Allegiance at all costs. What are we aligned with and what is
aligned with us?

Most days I can't shake my son no matter how many times I
duck into the bathroom. What am I doing with this kind of an
audience? As an introvert, it's hard for me not to attempt to dodge
the company. Then I think of the days he will not go where I go.
The days I will not know for certain where he is. In these days now

of a three-year-old shadow my hope is to lead him through the actions of my day to propel him toward actions of integrity later. So that even when we are not physically together, he will still "go where you go, Mom."

Maybe you don't have a three-year-old following your every move. Maybe you are single or don't have children and are reading this, thinking it doesn't apply. If that's the case, let me put it this way: what you do now affects what you will be doing later. I have made many decisions in my life without realizing the impact they would have on the future. Decisions for the right now, with little thought about where they would take me. If I do not bring awareness to my actions to understand how they are leading me, I will end up in a destination I might not desire.

I have aligned myself with people who have led me down different paths—some helpful, some harmful. You may not have someone following your every step, but are you following someone else's? Your choices matter—whether they are leading those around you … or they are leading you to or from your goals.

QUESTIONS

1. Are you aware of the power of your choices and how they affect your future goals?

2. Who are you "going where they go"?

3. Who is "going where you go"?

4. Would you act differently if someone were watching your decisions each day?

Is Death the End?

"O death, where is your victory? O death, where is your sting?"

1 Corinthians 15:55

THERE ARE SOME endings I have looked forward to. There are others I have dreaded—or worse, I didn't even see them coming. The end of a good book. The end of a relationship. The end of a graduate program. The end. All of us deal with endings in our own way. I like to think that over the years I have hardened myself toward endings, but even now as I sit down to write about them, my first instinct is to avoid the topic.

I want to tell you to look at endings as an opportunity. A chance for another beginning. The end to one thing makes space for the next. There is hope in the end. And there is. But I can't ignore the endings that seem cruel. I lost my friend Sarah when she was just twenty-nine years old. I hadn't seen her for a few months as we lived in different cities. I had just had my first child and he was three months old. I was visiting my parents in California, and Sarah and I planned to meet up, as this was where she currently lived. But we didn't. She was sick, and I put off seeing her until she felt better.

I was working out when the first call came. I didn't answer, and I didn't check the voicemail. I had showered and was holding my son when the second call came. It was a friend I didn't hear from often, and I answered, expecting a lighthearted life update. What I received was news of Sarah's death. I didn't see this ending coming. I cried so hard, my son broke out in tears, mirroring my grief. A baby felt the depth of my sorrow.

I'm a positive person, and I believe there is always good to be found. I'm still searching for the good that might have rippled from Sarah's death. I tell myself there must be a purpose for this ending. Is death the end? Is there hope, even in the deepest sorrow? In this ending I lean on a hope I cannot see. A heaven I cannot understand or imagine. A perspective that to die is not the end, but another beginning.

I've always loved fall. Even in Southern California the changes of autumn are palpable. Is it the light? Is it the slight dip in temperature? I'm not sure, but there is excitement that comes each October. Isn't it strange how hope can be born, even as I head into a season of death? Fall is a time when the earth turns inward. When I cannot see the beauty of green leaves or colorful petals. But I do not despair. I wrap myself in soft blankets and welcome the change.

Remember there is always hope, even when you are headed into a season where the beauty around you is not evident.

QUESTIONS

1. How do you feel about endings?

2. When has the end to something turned out to be good?

3. What has been a hard ending for you?

4. Do you see death as the end?

Waiting on God

God's Timing

Now Sarai, Abram's wife, had borne him no children. She had
a female Egyptian servant whose name was Hagar. And Sarai
said to Abram, "Behold now, the Lord has prevented me from
bearing children. Go in to my servant; it may be that I shall obtain
children by her." And Abram listened to the voice of Sarai. So,
after Abram had lived ten years in the land of Canaan, Sarai,
Abram's wife, took Hagar the Egyptian, her servant, and gave
her to Abram her husband as a wife. And he went in to Hagar,
and she conceived. And when she saw that she had conceived, she
looked with contempt on her mistress. And Sarai said to Abram,
"May the wrong done to me be on you! I gave my servant to your
embrace, and when she saw that she had conceived, she looked on
me with contempt. May the Lord judge between you and me!"

Genesis 16:1–5

GOD DOESN'T TELL me everything at once. Often, he doesn't give me much information to go on at all. I guess that's why they call it faith. In Genesis 15 God told Abram (later renamed Abraham) that he would father a nation. What? Abram is old, and so is his wife. They haven't had kids. It's a little late to start populating an entire nation. But nonetheless this is what God promises. In some ways it is a very descriptive promise; in other ways a lot of logistical details are left out. I don't know about you, but if I had just had a conversation with God about my future that held big plans that I was an integral part to, my first thought wouldn't be, *OK cool, God's got this.* My first thought would be, *How in the world am I going to make that happen?* I've just left a conversation with God, and immediately I'm focused on *me.*

With this in mind, I can relate to Sarai. As Abram shared the promise God has just made him, Sarai is likely thinking surely that promise can't extend to her. She can't be part of the plan. And like Sarai, I've dealt with infertility. I know the loss that can come when our bodies don't do what we hope they will. I can only imagine the pain Sarai felt when Abram came home and told her he was going to father a nation. Perhaps she was at a place where she had made peace with her infertility. Perhaps it was something she still didn't understand. Either way, she never considered herself part of God's plan. And so, she made her own plan.

I make my own plans daily. I'm so good at making plans, I can forget to even include God in them, let alone ask if they are in line with his plan. Whether God cares about all of our plans (like the order in which I do dishes, read the bible, exercise ...) is a deeper theological question than I'm ready to answer right now, but there is an argument to be made about the act of seeking God's plan before our own each day. It seems so silly sometimes to ask God what his plan is for my day. I'm doing little things. My time is spent dropping kids off and changing diapers. But when I stop asking God what his plan is, I start thinking it's all up to me. I am no longer leaning on the grace and power of God. I am doing things my way.

Sarai heard Abram would have a baby, and she didn't sit back and say, *Wow, I can't wait to see how that's going to happen.* Instead, she grabbed the closest fertile woman and said, *I can make this happen.*

How many times have you heard a promise from God and

attempted to take control of it? Stop making your own plans and expecting God to join in. Start seeking his plan first. If this becomes your starting point, when he comes with the inconceivable plan for your future, instead of asking, *How will I ever do that?* you will say, *I can't wait to see how God will make this happen.*

QUESTIONS

1. Do you seek God's plan ahead of your own?

2. Have you ever received a promise from God and tried to move forward instead of waiting on him?

3. Do you trust God's plan for your life?

You Cannot Stop God's Plan

And God said to Abraham, "As for Sarai your wife, you shall not call her name Sarai, but Sarah shall be her name. I will bless her, and moreover, I will give you a son by her. I will bless her, and she shall become nations; kings of peoples shall come from her." Then Abraham fell on his face and laughed and said to himself, "Shall a child be born to a man who is a hundred years old? Shall Sarah, who is ninety years old, bear a child?" And Abraham said to God, "Oh that Ishmael might live before you!" God said, "No, but Sarah your wife shall bear you a son, and you shall call his name Isaac. I will establish my covenant with him as an everlasting covenant for his offspring after him. As for Ishmael, I have heard you; behold, I have blessed him and will make him fruitful and multiply him greatly. He shall father twelve princes, and I will make him into a great nation. But I will establish my covenant with Isaac, whom Sarah shall bear to you at this time next year."

Genesis 17:15–21

I'M PRONE TO messing up. I don't like to admit this, but it's true. This shouldn't feel like a big confession, but it's still hard to say. Sometimes the fear of messing up can paralyze my actions. When faced with a hard decision, I'm tempted to stop and wait for a guarantee that's never coming. As I previously stated, I can also be so determined to make something happen that I stop asking God about his plan and just focus on my own. This is almost a guarantee of creating a mess.

I've always wanted to get married and have a family. This has been my plan for as long as I can remember. In my late twenties I started to see a lot of my friends pairing off. What did I do? I started dating the wrong guys. No, not those wrong guys ... just the wrong guys for me. I was trying to make anything work. Of course, I didn't realize it while I was doing it. I thought I was keeping an open mind. And, to some degree, that's how it would start. But there would always come a time when I knew the relationship was not the right one for me. And in that season, I wouldn't listen. I would continue. I wanted my plan more than God's plan. I didn't know God's plan, and that was the problem. There was no guarantee of marriage in my future. The fear of not knowing lead me to attempt to secure what I wanted over what God might have in store for me.

Abraham and Sarah messed up. It was a pretty big mess-up. Abraham heard a promise from God, that he would father a nation, and he and Sarah decided to make it happen. Well, that wasn't what God had intended. And in Genesis 17 God comes down to face the mess and reveal his plan of redemption.

Here is where I take comfort: My mess-ups are never too big. I cannot get in the way of God's plan. This doesn't mean that I should move blindly and without tact as I make decisions in the world. But it does mean I cannot let the fear of messing up stop me from making decisions in my life.

QUESTIONS

1. Do you trust God to be bigger than your mistakes?

2. Have you seen God's redemption in your life?

3. When have you stepped out in faith? Did you see God meet you there?

4. Have you ever stepped out in faith and been redirected by God?

For Such a Time as This

---

*"For if you keep silent at this time, relief and deliverance
will rise for the Jews from another place, but you and your
father's house will perish. And who knows whether you
have not come to the kingdom for such a time as this?"*

Esther 4:14

I AM NOT THAT important. But I want to be. I want my time
to matter. There is a struggle in my day to protect my time.
I rush from one activity to the next. Even as I try to write
this, there are three boys swirling around me, begging for my time.
It's easy in the commotion of my day to consider most moments
interruptions. There are many times in my day I consider my
children interruptions. They stand in the way of my productivity.
They are actively working against my desire for my house to be
clean. They are asking me questions while I am attempting to have
a quiet time. They are getting in the way of my importance.

I'm looking for the big moment. What I want is "for such a time
as this." I want to be important. And so, I find I often rush through
my day, shooing away the things I've deemed interruptions.

Many of us are not given that big moment. We're not faced
with a call to save a significant population of people because we
married a king. That's not our story. But just because the big
moment isn't on the docket for today doesn't mean our time doesn't

matter. Every moment in our life is an opportunity. God is calling to us every day. Each morning he is whispering to us, *"For such a time as this."* He longs for us to respond to his calling and see each day as a distinct moment that will never occur again. It's easy to miss. When raising young children, most days feel a bit like a scene from *Groundhog Day*. Wake up, survive, go to bed, and then do it all over again the next day. Man, is it easy for life to feel mundane right now.

But each day isn't the same; it is uniquely made by our Creator. It is distinct. Our challenge is to discover the opportunity in each day. Whether our "for such a time" is a big moment or small, it is deliberately placed in our path. It is a call from God, asking for a response.

By the way, the great thing (big or small) will happen without us. This is made perfectly clear in the first part of the passage, "For if you keep silent at this time, relief and deliverance will arise for the Jews from another place." God doesn't need us. He doesn't need our interaction to have his will accomplished. The big or small thing that we are being asked to act upon will happen just as it should, with or without us. We cannot stop it or screw it up.

If fear is stopping you from acting, rest in God's power. Your response to his request will be enough. And if you are too involved in seeking the big moment, so that you are missing the small one he is offering you, his plan will happen without you. God does not need you; he invites you.

So often I rush through the day. Working to get as much done as I can. Pining for importance. I'm missing it. I'm missing "for such a time as this." Are you?

QUESTIONS

1. Do you seek importance in your daily life? What does that look like?

2. What are the small moments God is offering to you? How can you change your response?

3. Have you experienced a time when God asked you to do something and you refused?

4. Did it happen without you?

5. Are you drawn to the big callings or the little ones?

The Right Time

Wait for the LORD; be strong, and let your heart take courage; wait for the LORD!

Psalm 27:14

FINDING THE RIGHT time usually means waiting. I've waited on a lot of things in my life. And each time I grew impatient as I was waiting, I would think something like, *I'd be OK with the waiting as long as I knew it was all going to work out.* I wanted assurance it was going to be OK.

In my late twenties I started to say to God, *I want to be married. It doesn't have to be now. I just want to know it's going to happen.* I didn't get married until more than four years later. I wanted to know what was going to happen years before anything actually did. What was going to happen was a bumpy road to marriage. I lost a friend in the process of gaining my husband. A friend who also wanted to date Ben, despite that not being his desire. Feelings were hurt, friendships were broken. If I had known the pain ahead in order to find the joy, I might have doubted God's plan. I might have rejected what was to come.

Waiting allows me to prepare for the unknown. It creates a yearning for what's to come, even when I must move through pain and disappointment to get there. Waiting forces me to trust God over myself. I cannot find the right time unless I identify the wrong time. That takes faith. As someone who likes to create her own destiny in the form of *action, action, action,* I continue to learn that when I pursue something outside of the right time, it will almost always blow up in my face.

How do I know it's the right time? I don't always. That is the mystery of God. He purposely doesn't give me the roadmap to my life. Can you imagine how much less exciting it would have been if I had known exactly who I would marry? And when? I would have missed the butterflies I felt on our first date, walking the streets of Chicago, sharing a Christmas coffee, wandering in and out of storefronts, looking at gifts for loved ones. I would have also skipped all the relationships ahead of meeting Ben and probably would have missed the growth that came from them, preparing me for marriage.

There is no room for hope if I already know. There is no dependence on God if he gives me the answers up front. God yearns for a relationship with me. And so, I investigate. I seek out wise counsel. I read God's Word. I pray. I identify when I clearly see it is the wrong time. The good news? There won't be just one "right time" in my life. I will have many opportunities to practice the discipline of waiting for the right time.

QUESTIONS

1. Have you been able to see when it is the right time for something in your life?

2. Do you want God to give you all the answers, or are you comfortable with the unknown?

3. How do you feel about waiting?

The Wrong Time

*The LORD is good to those who wait for him, to
the soul who seeks him. It is good that one should
wait quietly for the salvation of the LORD.*

Lamentations 3:25–26

FTER MY SECOND miscarriage, I did not get pregnant again for seven months. I had gotten pregnant immediately with the two babies I then lost, so this felt like a slap in the face. Not only could I not keep a baby alive—I now couldn't conceive. There were some months when this didn't bother me, and there were others when I was all too aware of the deficit. I was in a season of waiting that butted up to a previous season of mourning. It was painful.

Fertility aside, the months of waiting were also hard months for our family. We were in a state of transition in other areas and having trouble working well together. Ben and I couldn't seem to communicate effectively, which led to arguments and frustrations. It was a hard summer. In the midst of it all, I couldn't see God's plan clearly. But as we worked through some of our challenges (and came out a stronger team), I started to see the beauty in the losses we had suffered.

If I had not lost either of my earlier pregnancies, I would have been very pregnant in the midst of all the other challenges we were going through. If I had gotten pregnant during our hard summer, it might have added pressure to an already stressful time. I can see all this now. I can see God and his merciful plan. I can see the beauty of waiting on God's timing. I can see this on the other side of waiting. Sometimes it's hard to see clearly while you're waiting.

What happens when I don't wait well? I start to take things into my own hands. I make decisions outside of God's plan. I make mistakes. Sometimes it's hard to know if I am waiting well or not. And God can absolutely use my mistakes—he even knows I am going to make them before I do. But it can make life harder.

Have you lost track in your waiting? Have you settled for something that is less than what you are waiting for? It's easy to abandon waiting for a compromise. After all, there is no guarantee you will get what you want in this life. I know women who are lovely inside and out and have not met their husband. I know women who yearn for a baby and cannot get pregnant. Sometimes there is an end to your waiting. Sometimes there is not. You spend your life always waiting for something, whether it's a spouse, a baby, a career, a friendship, or anything else. If you can find a way to embrace the wait, you will be able to make patient decisions rather than impatient compromises.

QUESTIONS

1. How can you see failures in your life as opportunities rather than setbacks?

2. How do you identify when it is the wrong time for something?

3. Are you good at waiting?

That's Not How I Do It!

But he said to them, "You give them something to eat." They said, "We have no more than five loaves and two fish—unless we are to go and buy food for all these people." For there were about five thousand men. And he said to his disciples, "Have them sit down in groups of about fifty each." And they did so, and had them all sit down. And taking the five loaves and the two fish, he looked up to heaven and said a blessing over them. Then he broke the loaves and gave them to the disciples to set before the crowd. And they all ate and were satisfied.

Luke 9:13–17

But when the disciples saw him walking on the sea, they were terrified, and said, "It is a ghost!" and they cried out in fear. But immediately Jesus spoke to them, saying, "Take heart; it is I. Do not be afraid." And Peter answered him, "Lord, if it is you, command me to come to you on the water." He said, "Come." So Peter got out of the boat and walked on the water and came to Jesus. But when he saw the wind, he was afraid, and beginning to sink he cried out, "Lord, save me." Jesus immediately reached out his hand and took hold of him, saying to him, "O you of little faith, why did you doubt?"

Matthew 14:26–31

B EN AND I were newly engaged. We were eating our dinner one night that consisted of subs and mini bags of chips. As we finished, Ben graciously went to clean up our wrappers, crumpling them all together into one big trash pile. Without so much as a thought stopping me, I exclaimed (almost involuntarily): "That's not how I do it!" It was a passionate outcry and stopped us both in our tracks. Seeing that I had truly committed to showing my crazy, I then proceeded to explain to him that I would first neatly roll my sandwich wrapper and then place it inside the chip bag. At this point you are either nodding your head in agreement or shaking it in disgust. I know. It was absurd. I was instructing my future husband in how to throw away the trash in the appropriate manner, rather than simply thinking how nice it was that he was performing a service for me.

I wish I could say that was the only time in life or even marriage that I have exclaimed those words. But it's not. "That's not how I do it!" is a common phrase I find myself repeating over and over again. The two relationships I say it in most: Ben and God.

While in my marriage there are times where it is important to share how I do things and for what reason, it is also important to let Ben find his own way of doing things. I've learned over the years (and continue to learn) that how I do things is as unique as my fingerprint. But just as my routines can be my strength, they can also be my weakness.

I can't think of a time when I have told God, *That's not how I do it!* and been right. I cannot think of a time when God's plan has been substandard to mine. Still, I keep finding myself telling him how he should be doing things. The most grace-giving part of this is that even when I try to strong-arm my way into the picture with God, he always leads me back to his way.

The disciples are often confusing to me. They have God's son standing right in front of them, performing miracles: healing the sick, walking on water, multiplying food. And yet they still ask him why he is doing things the way he is doing them. They still question and doubt. It feels foolish and shortsighted, maybe even blind. But isn't that what I am doing when I shout at God that it should be done my way, not his? Aren't I picking up where the disciples left off by questioning his actions? And while I like to look back at those walking with Jesus and think, *How could you not see what was right before you?*, I'm looking through a lens of completion. I know the whole story. I have seen Christ's actions from birth to resurrection and can see on the other side how they all make sense. Of course, it's easy for me to judge. Yet, even while I know the whole story of my salvation, I am still exclaiming to God, *That's not how I do it!*

QUESTIONS

1. How are you telling God what to do?

2. How can you choose to obey rather than attempt to lead?

When It's Time to Stop Waiting

*"He has told you, O man, what is good; and what does
the LORD require of you but to do justice, and to love
kindness, and to walk humbly with your God?"*

Micah 6:8

SOMETIMES GOD ASKS me to wait for a long time. Waiting
is good. It creates patience and faith. When I wait, I look
forward to what I am waiting for. Waiting can bring out the
best or the worst in me. It can allow me to look forward to what
is to come, or it can foster resentment for what I do not have. The
tricky thing about waiting is, it can be unclear when I am meant
to stop waiting. If I am not careful, waiting can become a crutch.

How do you know if you are stuck in a pattern of waiting?
There are times when you need to stop waiting and start acting.
You're in a job you've dreamed of leaving for years. You're in a relationship that doesn't seem to be going anywhere. You want to get
healthy, but keep sitting on the couch rather than finding a gym.

Waiting can become a deterrent to action. You can get comfortable waiting for God to act, rather than taking a step of action
yourself. If that's the case … just say *yes*. Yes, to any and all opportunities that come your way.

When I was new in Chicago and desperately wanted friends,
I started saying yes. I went to all the events at my church. I made

myself have all the awkward conversations. I said yes to the invitations to other gatherings, where other awkward conversations had to be had. And then, eventually, the conversations stopped being awkward and started being meaningful. I found people I wanted to spend time with. I made friends. It didn't happen overnight, and it took putting myself in situations that made me uncomfortable. It absolutely required me to leave my couch. It forced me to stop waiting and start acting.

Sometimes it's hard to know when to wait and when to act. Sometimes I act when I shouldn't. Look at Micah 6—it is filled with action words. Even in seasons of waiting, I am not called to be passive. I am called to walk with God. When I am walking with God, I am able to more clearly see when he is asking me to wait and when he is calling me to move forward.

QUESTIONS

1. Have you ever been stuck in a time of waiting?

2. How did you end the time of waiting and step into action?

3. What have you been saying no to that you should start saying yes to?

Don't Forget the Journey

Are You Present?

Let all that you do be done in love.

1 Corinthians 16:14

WHEN I BECAME a mom, I lost a lot of personal space and time. With the addition of each child, I suddenly became aware of both the time I previously had and the time I was now losing all at once. Being a parent is not for the selfish at heart. I'm selfish, by the way. I am selfish with my time. I hoard time—collecting it, hiding it away. I resent when someone finds my stash of time and tries to claim some of it. This is what parenthood has revealed to me.

The problem with being a time hoarder is I can easily stop being present. If I'm focused on my time, I stop seeing beauty when I'm doing anything less than what I want to be doing. I'm focused on the list at hand, the things I have to get done in order to arrive at the thing I want to do. And I'm missing a lot.

I grew up in California. I never appreciated what it had to offer until I left, moving to Chicago, where I would live for ten years. Once I moved back to California, I was on a trip to the coast with my family, and I revisited a town I had lived in right after college. In some ways it looked the same, and in others it had obviously changed. What I was most hung up on were the things I wasn't sure about. Were they old or new? There was a mural painted on the side of a small older building, and its romantic Southwest depiction immediately captivated my imagination. I couldn't stop wondering, *Was it there all along? Had I just never noticed it?* I now realize, I miss the opportunity to appreciate so many things until I look back.

My life can feel complicated. It is filled with ups and downs, successes and failures. Sometimes these highs and lows are perfectly balanced, and sometimes they sway in one direction, tipping the scales. How do I stay present in a distracting world? I do all things with love. I know, I grimaced a bit when I wrote it, too. It sounds so glib. But stay with me for a minute. I may not be able to actually do all things with love, but I can attempt to. I can seek love in everything I do. Even in the moments when love is not evident, I can be looking. If I'm seeking love, I'm paying attention. No, I won't notice every detail of every day. But I will start to bring an awareness to my surroundings. Perhaps even noticing particulars that might otherwise have gone unnoticed. When I am able to see the beauty in the details of my day, I'm signaling to myself that I have succeeded at being present.

QUESTIONS

1. Are you present?

2. What distracts you throughout the day?

3. What do you think about doing all things with love?

What Do You Want to Remember?

Do not let your adorning be external—the braiding of hair and the putting on of gold jewelry, or the clothing you wear—but let your adorning be the hidden person of the heart with the imperishable beauty of a gentle and quiet spirit, which in God's sight is very precious.

1 Peter 3:3–4

GIVE ME ALL the fashion! When I was looking at colleges to apply to, I considered going to fashion school. That is, until my parents told me I had to get a liberal arts degree first. Four years later, a theology degree in hand, I still loved fashion. So much so that one of my jobs out of school was in costuming. I braid my hair, wear gold jewelry, and love creating the perfect outfit to match my mood.

So you can imagine this verse is not my favorite. Before I dive into what I take from 1 Peter, I want to be clear: There are some things in the Bible that were most likely written out of a cultural lens that may or may not be completely relevant to the present day. And while I struggle with some things the Bible says about women and countless other topics, I'm also choosing to squeeze every ounce of wisdom I can from it at any opportunity. I see this verse as an opportunity.

When I was twenty-eight, I gave up looking in the mirror for Lent. I was single and living alone. Forty days without seeing my reflection. I covered all the mirrors in my home and avoided even seeing my reflection in the toaster. As you can imagine, the first week of this was a steep learning curve. I learned to put my makeup on blindly. I dried my hair without seeing the finished product. And I never knew exactly how my outfits really looked. Pictures were taken of me during that time, and I never saw them. It was strange and wonderful all at the same time. Although I felt disoriented in the beginning of my mirror-fast, by the end I felt freed. Many times my perception of myself comes from a reflection. That minute I spend in front of a mirror can dramatically change my self-confidence. When Lent was over and my reflection returned, I found I was once again distracted by the person looking back at me. *Do my knees always look that way?* Seriously, this was a conversation I had with myself. I even went so far as to enlist a few friends in assessing my legs when we were out to dinner one night.

So often I get wrapped up in the presentation of my life. Do I know the "right" people at church? Are my kids behaving? How do my arms look? I care about what others think. I have my own expectations for my life. I don't think wearing jewelry or braiding my hair or buying a new pair of jeans is inherently evil. But pride is. When how I look becomes my idol, it robs me of my peace. It distracts me from the moment. I love clothes because they are yet one more creative outlet that allows me to express myself. But if I could focus more on how I feel rather than how I look, the moments and memories would be so much sweeter.

QUESTIONS

1. Are you distracted by worrying about your appearance?

2. How would a day without mirrors make you feel? What about forty days without mirrors?

3. What is a favorite memory from the past year? Why?

4. Is how you looked in the memory from question three important? Does it enhance the memory, detract from the memory?

Patience in the Process

For I am sure that neither death nor life, nor angels nor rulers,
nor things present nor things to come, nor powers, nor height
nor depth, nor anything else in all creation, will be able to
separate us from the love of God in Christ Jesus our Lord.

Romans 8:38–39

I REMEMBER WHEN I was fifteen, all I could think about was getting my driver's license. I was obsessed with driving. I can clearly remember thinking that if I passed my driver's test, I would have everything I needed to be happy. I took my test the day I turned sixteen and passed. That was it. I got my driver's license, and I was happy—for a while.

In my late twenties, I started to realize that I was single. Well, yes, of course I knew I was single. Having broken up with my college boyfriend at twenty-six, I was all too happy to be single. But, as time wore on and I didn't seem to be meeting anyone else, my situation started to feel a bit unappealing. There were years when I cried out to God, asking what the heck was going on. And in that time, I thought if I could only meet the right person and get married, that would be everything I needed to be happy. I got married at thirty-two, and I was happy—for a while. (I feel the need to clarify that I'm happily married. But marriage has not protected me from all future unhappiness.)

There have been lots of things I've assigned my happiness to: test scores, college, friends, weight, clothes, children. The list goes on and is quite embarrassing when I come face-to-face with it. It will come as no surprise that none of these things has managed to make me permanently happy. None of these things has solved all of my problems. And yet, this seems to be what we do (I hope I'm not the only one). We look toward something that we think is going to change us, the thing that is going to complete us. And I would guess that, like me, you are left with an accomplishment hangover.

Accomplishment hangover: the letdown when real life continues on with the good, bad and ugly after we have achieved a significant goal in our life.

How do we combat the accomplishment hangover?

- *We recognize that no one thing is going to fix everything.* Guess what? After I reached every single one of my happiness goals, I didn't stay happy forever. The wonder of whatever it was wore off when I was no longer basking in the glow of achievement. I was just back to being me. If we are able to take a step back from our goals to see them for what they are, we are able to disarm them. And by disarming them, we are able to enjoy the time it takes to reach our goals just as much as actually achieving them.

- *We celebrate every moment.* Doesn't that sound impossible? There have been "happiness goals" I haven't achieved. There are jobs I didn't get. There are guys (lots of guys) who didn't want to date me. And man, that was embarrassing and painful at the time. But it was also right. If we can look back and see how missed goals have helped us, we are able to look forward to the uncertainty and recognize that it will be OK. It will. It may not always feel like it, but it will.

The only true finish line is God. We are all going to die. Until we do, we will have good moments and bad moments. We will achieve and fail. If we can accept that none of our failures or successes will change our finish line—an eternity with God—then we can start to actually embrace all parts of the process rather than just checking off the next item on our list. I'm still working on this. I'm still working on celebrating my moments of failure as well as my times of success. But the less I depend on these small goals to produce some sort of permanent happiness in my life, the more I am able to have patience in the process.

QUESTIONS

1. Have you ever attached your happiness to achieving a goal?

2. Once you achieved it, how long did it make you happy?

3. If God is our true destination, how does this change your goals and behaviors today?

How You View Your Story

The Lord is my shepherd; I shall not want. He makes me lie down in green pastures. He leads me beside still waters. He restores my soul. He leads me in paths of righteousness for his name's sake. Even though I walk through the valley of the shadow of death, I will fear no evil, for you are with me; your rod and your staff, they comfort me. You prepare a table before me in the presence of my enemies; you anoint my head with oil; my cup overflows. Surely goodness and mercy shall follow me all the days of my life, and I shall dwell in the house of the Lord forever.

Psalm 23:1–6

YOU'VE PROBABLY PICKED up on this by now, but I'm writing this book in the middle of a pandemic. It's not the ideal time to do this. But it's happening. The temptation some of you may have is to assume that I have it all together. But I don't. My life has hit all the phases during this time. All of the pre-pandemic routines have been shattered, and we have run through several versions of attempted schedules that work and then suddenly stop working. There are days I am my best self, wife and mom. Then there are days that I yell at myself, Ben or the kids. I'm overwhelmed a lot, and some days I'm just trying to survive.

It occurred to me recently that I could look at my day as an obstacle to endure or a story to embrace. When I find myself in the obstacle mentality, I fight the day. I get frustrated at the kids for being ... well, kids. I get bogged down. I worry about things not looking the way I want them to look. But as I've started looking back at the frustrations of each day, I've noticed that what, in the moment, felt like an obstacle, can be rather funny in the retelling.

Yesterday I was trying to avoid a meltdown from my oldest because I wouldn't let him watch one more show. In desperation I suggested a game of hide-and-seek. A five-year-old, three-year-old, one-year-old and me—what could possibly go wrong? As I counted and the older two hid, I heard screaming. My oldest was so irritated that his brother kept following him to all of his hiding spots. I finally, mid count, had to pull his younger brother aside and tell him where to hide. Crisis averted.

We then switched, and my middle son was now the seeker. As I attempted to run to find a spot, my oldest son kept following me around. He was doing the exact thing his younger brother had just done that had driven him to frustration. The giggles started deep within; I couldn't help it. We were bumping into each other as I tried to dodge my son and hide without him. I'm big; there aren't that many places I can blend in. We both finally pathetically hid in the same room, and all I could think, as we were doomed to be found quickly, was that these are the two options clearly displayed in a game of hide-and-seek: scream in frustration or take a deep breath and find the laughter. To walk in the valley of the shadow of death and know God is with me. He is with me in the frustration as well as the joy. When I recognize this, it transforms my perspective in each moment.

The best days are the ones when I don't have to wait to gain perspective, when I can be in the midst of the obstacle and simultaneously celebrate the telling of my story. When I keep this reminder close, the worst moments have the opportunity to become the most entertaining.

QUESTIONS

1. What are the obstacles in your day?

2. Does knowing God is your shepherd change how you view the obstacles in life?

3. Has there ever been something that really upset you that later became funny in the retelling?

4. How do you view your story?

You Will Miss This

"When a woman is giving birth, she has sorrow because
her hour has come, but when she has delivered the
baby, she no longer remembers the anguish, for joy that
a human being has been born into the world."

John 16:21

A S A MOTHER of young children, one of the most common phrases I hear from others is, "Enjoy this phase because it goes by quickly, and one day you will miss it." I usually smile and agree. But the truth is, I'm not sure I will miss all of it. Will I miss sleepless nights nursing a baby, potty training, a child who only wants Mom to put him to bed at the end of a sixteen-hour day? Will I miss a screaming, hysterical temper-tantrum or a picky eater? Vomit in the crib? Nope. Parenthood is hard. It is a forfeit of my previous independence. It is to take up the cross and serve someone who poops in his pants or, if I am lucky, poops in the toilet but still requires me to wipe his butt.

Still, there must be some truth to the statement. Clichés exist because they started out as a truth commonly acknowledged. Here's what I think people actually mean when they say, "You will miss this":

- *I will miss the memory, rather than the reality.* Every time

I birthed a child, it was painful. It was messy. It required stitches and nurses who were kind enough to see me at my most vulnerable and help clean me up. It was not a Hallmark movie. It was not something I cared to invite a photographer into, let alone ask my husband to document with a cell phone camera. And then, at the end of birthing, I would hold a small package that utterly ruined me, in the best possible way. A beating heart, bone of my bone, wrapped in skin, knit together by two who created this one. A warm creation that won't latch properly, has its nights and days mixed up, pees on me between diaper changes, and altogether seems to have the mission in life to never let me sleep again. If I make a pros and cons list on the entire birthing process (and I would argue on pregnancy, too), the cons may seem to stack up. The magic of it all is that I forget the pain. I forget the pain of childbirth. I forget the sleepless fog. I forget what the struggles actually feel like. That's good. It's a blessing to look back and remember the warmth over the ache.

- *I will miss my children needing me.* Do I love brushing their teeth? Nope. I don't even really like brushing my own teeth. I just heard the other day that we as parents are supposed to help our kids brush their teeth until the age of eight, or something crazy like that. Eight years of brushing another person's teeth?! Ugh. No one told me this small detail when I was family planning. And don't forget I am doing this twice a day! This is only one of the many things they need me to do for them. One day I will say, "I miss the days of their little teeth and singing to them while brushing." It seems crazy now, but the truth is, what I will really miss is them needing me. Arguably the biggest part of child raising is equipping my kids to be self-sufficient.

And while this seems like a desirable goal throughout the first eighteen-ish years, the irony is that when they finally don't need me anymore, there will be loss. There will be dramatic displacement of my identity. And I will miss being needed. I will miss being relevant.

- *I will miss when I had the illusion of protecting them.* Dare I say *control?* It is my drug of choice. And while parenting young children has painfully shown me just how little control I have, it also has fed some of that need. These kids are dependent on me. I am their first line of defense. They are not in the world driving, making their own decisions. They do not go anywhere I don't know about. I can kiss a scraped knee and heal it. I can tell them they are safe and they still believe me. One day these pieces of my DNA will be in the world, driving a car, going to college, marrying, and starting their own family—and I will not be able to protect them. I will be an observer of their choices. I will not be asked permission. And as much as that is right, I know it will hurt for a bit.

I struggle to be present. I look toward the *next.* I look toward relief. And while a sense of future and momentum is healthy to keep me moving forward, it can also distract me from the present. I may not miss all of what comes with raising young children, but I still recognize the fleeting nature of time. Perhaps this is not your plight; this doesn't just apply to parenting toddlers. It is easy to want to rush through a season that feels taxing. You might be attempting to climb the professional ladder. You are simply tolerating the current role you employ at your work. And while you may not miss the grunt work you must do now to succeed, there is still value in each job title that stands between you and the position you are wishing to attain. Take stock of the season you are currently in.

The temptation can be to look so far ahead in any circumstance that you miss the *now*.

QUESTIONS

1. Has there been a time you tried to rush through something you now miss?

2. What would you have done differently?

3. How can you apply that to the time you are in now?

Faith in What You Cannot See

*We look not to the things that are seen but to the
things that are unseen. For the things that are seen are
transient, but the things that are unseen are eternal.*

2 Corinthians 4:18

I HAVE A SMALL vegetable garden. I've had it for a couple of years now. I was told when I started this garden to beware of mint. It tends to take over and is very hard to get rid of. Nonetheless, I planted mint last year. I like mint. It smells fresh, it's easy to grow, and while I don't put it in a lot of things, I found my oldest son would break off a leaf and chew on it when playing outside. Slowly but surely the mint started to spread. What started out in a small patch in my planting bed creeped its way between the kale, and even started popping up with the strawberries. Eventually it became evident: something had to be done. So, a few days ago I started weeding out the mint. What I found was a network under the soil that was overwhelming. Just when I thought I had ripped up the last of the mint, I would dig to plant something new and find a robust matrix of mint roots infiltrating most of the garden. I had no idea! Even today, as I went to plant, I stuck my shovel in the soil and hit yet another mint root.

The mint in my garden is feeling eternal right now. Of course it's not, but it serves as a good reminder that just because we can't see something doesn't mean it's not there. I have a hard time with the fact that we can't see God. Sure, we can see his works in our lives when we are firing on all cylinders. But I can't see God as a physical being. Since I was a child, I have had a conversation with God that goes something like this: *Please just show yourself to me right now. Just this one time. Come to me in physical form.* This hasn't happened, yet. I have a hard time picking God over almost anything else I can see. Faith is a daily discipline for me.

Just like the mint, God is present, beyond my vision, working in my life. When I have faith in what I cannot see, I don't become rigid, holding tight to what I can see. There have been many paths in my life that would have led to dead ends, had I stayed fixed on what I could see. But my faith in what I can't see has allowed many of my dreams to adapt as new opportunities have revealed themselves. Faith in an unseen God allows for faith in an unseen future. It's OK for the dream to change as I am led down God's path for my life. It's great to grow past what I initially hoped for. Faith in an unseen God allows for fluidity in my life. It allows me to hold my plans loosely and accept change. When I have faith outside of my own capabilities, in an invisible God, I am fortified when the things that I can see fail me.

QUESTIONS

1. Do you believe God is at work in your life, even when you can't see him?

2. How do you have faith in a God you cannot physically see?

3. Have the things you could see ever failed you?

4. Have you ever had to move forward on faith? What happened?

Are We There Yet?

*The LORD will keep your going out and your coming
in from this time forth and forevermore.*

Psalm 121:8

I T'S THE AGE-OLD phrase spoken by every child under the age of twelve when on a long journey: "Are we there yet?" And, as every parent knows, this innocuous phrase wouldn't be so triggering, if it were spoken just once. It's the three hundred times after the first one that make it so obnoxious. Now that I have children, I realize how absurd this question is. When I am driving in the car (this does seem to be the most common situation for this phrase), I stop when I arrive at the chosen destination. Never has my destination been the middle of a freeway, surrounded by other speeding cars. Never has my destination been a red light. And yet, the question still pops up at the most obviously incorrect times. Of course we aren't there yet!

So why do they ask? Well, to start with, children don't know what we know. Sometimes they know the destination. Sometimes they know what it looks like. Sometimes they are familiar with the journey. But often they don't know the way or the destination. Most can't tell time and some can't adequately see out of the window. As kids we are excited for the destination. We are anxious for the next big event. We are impatient. As adults we grow out of this question when riding in the car, yet we continue to ask, "Are we there yet?" constantly throughout our days.

There are a lot of moments in my day that I view as filler—I'm simply passing the time. There are so many times I am asking God, "Are we there yet?" There are many days I am racing to the finish line. It is easy in the midst of days that feel repetitive or aimless to wish the time away. There are many days in my life that I have wished to speed through, whether because there was something exciting on the horizon or because life felt monotonous or even painful.

I miss things when I am focused on "Are we there yet?" I miss small and big moments. I don't always get "there," the place I am yearning to be, for years. Sometimes I get "there," and it's not the destination I hoped for. What lies ahead should propel me forward; it should give me hope. But where I am now should not be cast aside. It should not be discarded. Stop asking God, *Are we there yet?* and start recognizing that the journey is just as important as the destination.

QUESTIONS

1. Do you ask God, "Are we there yet?"

2. Are you impatient in the quiet moments?

3. How can you embrace the small moments between the big ones?

A Time For

A Time for Self-Care

---

*Do not be conformed to this world, but be transformed by the
renewal of your mind, that by testing you may discern what is
the will of God, what is good and acceptable and perfect.*

Romans 12:2

*A joyful heart is good medicine, but a
crushed spirit dries up the bones.*

Proverbs 17:22

I OPENED UP MY computer to write today and laughed at myself.
It's been a morning. Nothing crazy has happened. It's just been
one of those days where my emotions feel big. I finally huffed
off to my room to attempt to get away from all the people in my
house. Frankly, I have a bad attitude. I complained to a friend that
I'm doing all the things to attempt to get more time freed up in my
day, and it just isn't giving me the results I'd hoped for. And then
I saw *self-care* written in front of me, on my computer screen, as
the next topic to tackle for this book. *Self-care, like that's an option
right now.*

The thing is, I think of myself as rather good at self-care. The
definition of this can be drastically different from person to person.
So it's tricky to identify clearly what your self-care is going to be.
And truthfully, what constitutes self-care for myself changes from

season to season in my life. And so, I'm finding myself reevaluating what self-care is to me in this season of quarantining with a family of five.

While I can't tell you what your self-care method of choice should be, I can attempt to tell you how to identify if you are successfully incorporating self-care into your life. I can try to steer you closer to finding what self-care is for you. Let's start here. Stop. Right now, close your eyes, sit back, and take a deep breath. How do you feel? Do you feel relaxed and present? Do you feel anxious? Is this exercise even now just another item on your to-do list for today? Take inventory of your body tension, your posture. Is your mind having trouble slowing down? Are you angry or irritated? I suspect you know if you are doing a good job at self-care. It will be evident in your mind and body posture when you simply slow down or stop and take notice.

I was recently given a day "off." Ben very sweetly told me to take the day to myself to recharge. I loaded up a bag filled with books, my computer, a bathing suit and anything else that sounded fun. I can become paralyzed by free time very quickly. How will I decide between all the things I want to do? But on this day, I simply packed a bag of options and got in the car with my sister-in-law to take a staycation at her house (after weeks of making sure we were all doing the same safety practices, our families had all gathered together at my parents' home). I didn't end up using all the things in my bag—there wasn't enough time. Instead I ended up writing and going for a short walk. It wasn't glamorous. But it did fill me up. I ended that day feeling centered and grateful.

Are you currently living with a joyful heart or a crushed spirit? Most of you don't have the time or luxury to take a day off. You have busy lives. So how do you find the time for self-care? Make a list of things that fill you up. All the small and big things. Keep that list close. Think about what you would pack in your bag for a day away from your life. Now choose one thing from that bag—reading a book, working out, sitting in the sun, five minutes of quiet. I'm not here to tell you that it's easy to incorporate self-care into your life. I'm here to tell you that it's incredibly hard for some of us, but it is important.

QUESTIONS

1. Are you living with a joyful heart or a crushed spirit?

2. Are you good at self-care?

3. Do you know what fills you up?

4. If you had an afternoon off, what would you do?

5. How can you incorporate self-care into your routine?

A Time for Serving

And he sat down and called the twelve. And he said to them, "If anyone would be first, he must be last of all and servant of all."

Mark 9:35

Let each of you look not only to his own interests, but also to the interests of others.

Philippians 2:4

I WANT TO HELP others—when it's interesting to me. I want to help others—on my own time, at my own convenience. I'm good at deciding when it's the right time to serve. I'm also good at being too busy to serve. As I read through Bible verses, focused on serving, I am struck by how unglamorous serving comes off in the Bible. God seems to be asking me to serve, not when it works for my schedule and my interests, but when it is needed.

But I'm too busy! Seriously. Insert my list of excuses here: I'm a mom of young children, I have a husband who travels for work, and I'm just trying to find time for all the everyday things in my life. I love to offer a helping hand when it's convenient, but if I'm being honest, it's not convenient a lot of the time. When it comes to serving, I'm inclined to give myself a pass. I can rationalize away the need to serve quite easily.

What does it look like to serve others in the way God asks me to? God isn't inviting me to serve when I want to. He is asking me to serve when the need arises. God is asking that I look beyond myself—to see the needs of the people around me. This may mean looking at a friend's passion for how they serve and asking to be a part of it. This may mean seeing a need in my community and, despite my busyness, offering to help.

Recently, I started making masks for the homeless. I taught myself how to sew several years ago and had some extra fabric that had no purpose—and so it began. After several rounds of sewing, I calculated that each mask takes approximately thirty minutes to make. This doesn't sound like a lot of time. But when you are making batches of masks—usually ten at a time—it adds up. There have been many moments in constructing these masks that I have wanted to spend my time in some other way. It has not been convenient. This sacrifice of my time to serve others has been a reminder to me that a small action or gesture has potential. There is no perfect time or way to serve. The needs will likely always outweigh the resources. But simply showing up with a willing heart, not only serves the intended recipient, but also reminds me: It's not about what I can do; it's about what Jesus can do through me.

I'm not asking you to radically change your schedule and overload it with service. I'm asking, what does it mean to look beyond your own interests? What might come from looking inward less and reaching out more to serve those around you?

QUESTIONS

1. How do you currently serve?

2. Do you need to serve more or less?

3. Do you serve when it's convenient or when the need arises?

4. What has been your best experience serving?

A Time for Accepting Help

And he answered, "You shall love the Lord your God with all your heart and with all your soul and with all your strength and with all your mind, and your neighbor as yourself."

Luke 10:27

TWO SUMMERS AGO, I got sick. It came on suddenly, and before I knew it, I was curled up on the couch with a fever of 103.5. As so often happens when crisis strikes (and by *crisis,* I mean fire-alarm chirping in the middle of the night or child getting pink eye), Ben was out of town. The silver lining was that he had also taken our two older boys with him. So that left me and the newborn an opportunity for some mother-son bonding. It was lovely … until it was not. And the *not* hit hard. Quickly realizing I was going down fast, I reached out to notify the outside world. I was a bit concerned about someone out there simply making sure I was able to surface enough to care for the baby.

I'm not good at asking for help. I'm even worse at accepting it. The only two people I feel comfortable receiving help from are my husband and my mom, neither of whom were in town at the time. So before I went to bed on a Thursday night, I fortified with as much Advil and Tylenol as my body would tolerate and texted a friend. I simply told her I was pretty ill and said I'd like to text her at the night feeding and in the morning, just so someone was tracking that I was able to get out of bed to care for the baby.

Friday, the next morning, she was at my door, caring for both of us. Saturday morning, she was back. Saturday afternoon, my brother and sister-in-law came to do the same. And another friend dropped off magazines and my favorite coffee order (the best medicine).

Sometimes I have to accept help. It's not always easy to accept, or even ask for it. But my resistance to ask for help does not negate my need for it. It may be in a big or a little way. I don't need to always know all the answers or be self-reliant. My inability to accept help actually takes away the opportunity for someone else to love their neighbor. While I feel like I'm being considerate of other people's time, my selfish desire to be self-reliant can also turn into a fault.

Think about a time when you have been able to help someone else. There have been many times in my life when I have seen someone struggling and have been eager to alleviate their burden. Just as I wish for others to accept my help, I must also learn to accept the help of those around me.

Questions

1. How do you feel about getting help?

2. How do you feel when you are able to help others?

3. How do you think you love your "neighbor" well?

4. How could you improve loving your "neighbor"?

5. Where can you ask for or accept help today?

A Time for Health

Or do you not know that your body is a temple of the Holy Spirit within you, whom you have from God? You are not your own, for you were bought with a price. So glorify God in your body.

1 Corinthians 6:19–20

MY SENIOR YEAR of high school I stopped eating. I would skip breakfast and lunch and finally satiate my hunger at dinner. Having spent a large portion of my childhood overweight, I had tried different diets in an attempt to lose the weight. Sometimes I would succeed, but most times I would end up back where I started, feeling like a failure. I knew I didn't look like most of my peers, and it led me to believe there was something wrong with me.

I can't remember how I got the idea to cut my caloric intake by skipping meals, but I rationalized it was OK because after all, I needed to lose weight. And I did. By the end of the school year, I had dropped about thirty pounds. Now the size of an average girl, still a bit thicker than I preferred, I started eating again my freshman year of college, and despite continuing to be aware of my caloric intake, I thought little about my previous year's "diet." Though I never gained back those thirty pounds that I lost in my senior year of high school, the pattern continued to some degree several more times throughout college, and each time I had a reason why I was justified in my food choices.

There was no big awakening moment to push me past the abuse I was inflicting on myself—physically and emotionally. It was a slow shift to learning my worth is not connected to my size. It took time to recognize my body was not something to be at odds with but instead something to value as God's creation. I wish I could pinpoint when I released my unhealthy views of my body, but the truth is, to some degree they are still hiding in the shadows most days. Most likely, I will always think I can lose five more pounds. I will always think I could be in better shape, a smaller size. While my days of restricting food are far behind me, it is easy to see that I still work to see my body as a dwelling place for the Holy Spirit. While time has changed my relationship with my view of my body, it takes a trust and intimacy with God to fight off the unhealthy temptations of the past.

Our health is important—mentally and physically. How we treat our bodies is a reflection of our relationship with God. We are stewards of our physical and emotional states while we are here on earth. We are not meant to all have the same shape, color or physical ability. There is no one-size-fits-all when it comes to how we care for our bodies. But we are called to care for them. We are meant to nurture our bodies as a way of honoring God.

QUESTIONS

1. How do you take care of your body?

2. Do you make health a priority?

3. What do you think God wants for your health?

4. Have you ever abused your body? What helped you stop the abuse?

A Time for Love

Above all, keep loving one another earnestly,
since love covers a multitude of sins.

1 Peter 4:8

No MARRIAGE IS perfect. No person will fix whatever you think needs fixing. But the right person can make life a lot more fun. It's easy, in the chaos of life, to overlook how Ben and I spend our time together. Most nights it's easier to sit in front of the TV and not even care what we're watching. All I want to do at the end of a long day is tune the world out. I want to sit and shut my brain off. Some nights we do this; many nights we do this. While I am in support of us, as parents, surviving different seasons, I am also aware that our love should not be put on hold, no matter the season.

When we were in therapy several years ago (it was after that particularly hard summer that I talked about earlier), our therapist suggested that Ben and I make a list of thirty things our spouse could do or already did that made us feel loved. She explained that oftentimes couples attempt to show their spouse love, but it goes unfelt or unnoticed. With a list of specific examples of how to show Ben love, I could easily reference it throughout the week to strengthen our bond. At first each of us was eager to get home and start creating our lists. The first ten items poured themselves out on the page. Then as I hit twenty, I started to have a harder time coming up with things. I had to get creative; I had to really think about how I feel loved. As I write this, I'm realizing that I'm not sure where I put Ben's list, evidence that making time for love, even when it's given to you in list form, can be hard to do.

There have been many times in my life before marriage, when I put love on the back burner. Not every season in a single person's life is meant for romance. But there is a time for love. It's easy to want to avoid love. In order to give and receive love, I must be vulnerable. I must give up some of the control. I can tell you from experience, it doesn't always work out. People get hurt. When a relationship doesn't work out, it can be messy—that's because there is so much on the line.

God calls us to love. If you are married, are you taking your spouse for granted? Ben and I have continued to go on dates throughout our marriage. It's not always easy. We don't always feel like it. But we know to grow our relationship, we must put in the time. Not everyone is called to marriage. If you are single, what season are you in? Are you avoiding love because you refuse to be vulnerable? Are you seeking opportunities to love those around you? Take an honest assessment. Whether it's with a spouse, a partner or family member, make time for love.

QUESTIONS

1. Have you made time for love in your life?

2. How do you show love?

3. If you are single, how could you show love to those in your life right now?

4. If you are married, what is one action you could do today to show your spouse love?

5. How do you feel love? Make a list of actions that someone can do to show you love.

A Time for Listening

*The way of a fool is right in his own eyes,
but a wise man listens to advice.*

Proverbs 12:15

I ALWAYS HATED GROUP projects in school. Inevitably someone ended up doing most of the work. People didn't agree. There was a lot of wasted time trying to sort out who would do what. It always felt like a lot of work which yielded few results. And then I got married. My marriage is one big group project.

We needed an outdoor dining table. Ben and I wanted to have enough seating in our backyard that we could not only fit our family of five but also comfortably include friends or family to join us for outdoor gatherings. When Ben first told me that he wanted to make a table and showed me sketches, I was skeptical. I know he's talented. I know he's capable. But I just didn't catch the vision. It wasn't my vision for what I wanted. As is recommended in marriage, even though I didn't see what Ben saw, I supported him in his endeavor. What a surprise when it was finished—I loved it!

When I embrace Ben's perspective, I'm embracing living outside of a life of doing it my way. I'm learning patience, persistence, communication and humility. Now, as I look back, I realize that group projects are not really about the material, but more about preparing us for all the people we will run into throughout our lives. Some will want to do the work the way we do. Others will have a completely different approach. Some will just show up in time to put their name on the paper. What matters is learning to work well with others. In doing so, I learn to listen to others.

There are many times that I don't have the same point of view as those around me. Whether it's Ben, my children or a friend, it can be easy to get stuck in my own perspective. I wonder how many beautiful backyard tables I've missed out on because I was more concerned with what I wanted than with supporting some-one else's vision.

QUESTIONS

1. How are you at working with others?

2. Do you listen to those around you?

3. Practice active listening this week, stop worrying about what you are going to say next, and simply hear what the person talking to you is saying.

4. Has there ever been a time when you gained insight by listening to someone you didn't agree with?

A Time for Friendship

Two are better than one, because they have a good reward for their toil. For if they fall, one will lift up his fellow. But woe to him who is alone when he falls and has not another to lift him up! Again, if two lie together, they keep warm, but how can one keep warm alone? And though a man might prevail against one who is alone, two will withstand him—a threefold cord is not quickly broken.

Ecclesiastes 4:9–12

IT CAN BE hard to make friends. When I was starting the seventh grade, we moved and I started a new school. I didn't know how to make friends. I was a good student and (I think) well liked, but I couldn't seem to find friends. One day, after finishing eating my lunch in the library alone, I sat down on a bench near the courtyard where most students hung out during the lunch hour. Before I knew it, tears started slipping down my cheeks. A group of girls nearby noticed and asked what was wrong. In arguably one of my most pathetic high school moments I exclaimed, "I have no friends!" They attempted to console me and invited me to sit with them. And I did. But for some unknown reason to me, they didn't really become my friends. I would see them at school but never really felt that I belonged.

Since high school I have had many opportunities to make friends—college, graduate school, attending a new church, moving to a new city. Each time that I have been thrown back into the deep end, seeking friendship, I have learned it takes time to make friends. Every time I have been placed in a situation where I desire establishing friendship, it has felt daunting.

When I moved back to California four years ago, I knew I was about to start the process of making friends all over again. I had good friends in my life, just not in California. I knew it would take work. I knew it would take faith that a stranger can become a confidant. I knew it would take time. And it did. The first year we lived here I still very much felt I didn't have friends to truly turn to. I didn't have people who knew me or cared. And then, a little more time passed. I put myself in situations to spend time with people I still considered more stranger than friend. And then, a little more time passed, and strangers became acquaintances. And then, a little more time passed, and I realized I had invested in people around me who had started as strangers and now were friends.

Not everyone that I've attempted to invest in has become my friend. It's not as simple as that. There is no tried and true formula for friendship. But I have learned over time that when I show up with honesty and a willingness to sift through the discomfort of being unfamiliar with someone, often friendship grows.

There are also friendships that we lose over time. Keeping friends takes time. Remember my friend Mary from college? While we're still friends, we rarely speak. The reason being—we don't have the time. She lives in the Chicago suburbs with four children of her own, and I'm across the country with my own busy life. Sometimes friendships fade for no better reason that a lack of time to invest or being in a different stage of life that makes it harder to connect. This sad reality does not take away from the time Mary and I spent together (clearly, I owe a lot of physical transformation to her). My point is simply this: friendships are fed by the time I give them.

When I read Ecclesiastes 4, I look back at the chord of

friendship that Mary and I created in college. We made each other stronger—at least I know Mary made me stronger. The strength of my friendships in college was that we were are all experiencing similar things at the same time. In so many ways it was community at the purest level—living together, eating together, learning together. There were other friendship chords as well that I built in college—sorority sisters, fellow classmates. Each of these chords was slowly broken as we exited that specific time in our lives. But as I look back throughout my life, each time one friendship bond has weakened there has been another to take its place.

When I look at friendship through the lens of time, I can more clearly see that, like so many things, friendship takes time. It takes showing an interest in the people around me. It takes many uncomfortable conversations and meet-ups before I feel I belong. I have made many friends over the years. But the relationships that have stood the test of time are with the friends I have continued to find time to invest in.

QUESTIONS

1. Who are currently some of your closest friends? How long have you been friends with them?

2. Have you ever been lonely? If so, what helped end the loneliness?

3. Have you ever noticed someone who seemed lonely? What did you do?

4. Do you make time for friendship?

A Time for God

Pray without ceasing.

1 Thessalonians 5:17

I STRUGGLE WITH FINDING the right amount of time to devote to God. Even admitting that here on paper makes me cringe. If I believe God is the Creator of the universe, if I believe he sent his only Son to save us from our sins, why are there seasons where I simply am too busy for God? In my best spiritual life, I have 20–30 minutes every morning when I am able to sit somewhere quiet and do a study, read the Bible, write reflections, and pray. In my best spiritual life, I do this daily. In my best spiritual life, I leave this time feeling centered and close to God.

So how do I get so derailed? Somewhere along the way I have created a set of rules for what it looks like to successfully spend time with God. There must be no distractions. It should be early in the day. I must connect deeply with the words I am reading. It should be a certain amount of time. If I'm interrupted or distracted, it doesn't count. In creating guidelines for myself, I have also created roadblocks to spending time with God. If I don't have enough time to fit it all in perfectly, I won't do any of it at all. I put God on a shelf. And I only take him down when it fits into my day the way I want it to.

The problem is, even in my best spiritual life, when I am doing the daily work, when I am spending the time every day reading his Word and praying, I've still got it wrong. On the days when I avoid time with God because I don't think I can do it the "right" way with all my focus, I am doing it wrong. God doesn't want 20–30 minutes of daily enlightenment and prayer. He doesn't want me to save him for the quiet hours of the morning when there are no distractions. He wants all of it. He wants all of me.

Pray without ceasing. What does that look like? It looks like seeking God in all the moments of my day: quiet, loud, busy, boring. To dialogue daily with God. To bring him into my actions. To allow him to soften my heart. At the store. Changing a diaper. Driving.

This is not to suggest I quit pursuing time in the Word and time in prayer. Instead, it is to realize that when I limit my time with God to the perfect quiet time, I limit my invitation to him to enter every part of my life. What if I pursued my quiet time despite how complete it would be? What if I saw those 20–30 minutes in my day as just one of the many conversations I'm having with God? I wouldn't avoid prayer because there wasn't enough time. I wouldn't worry about the perfect Bible passage to motivate or change my heart. I would see it for what it was—one of the many moments with him. I might start to pray without ceasing.

QUESTIONS

1. What does your ideal quiet time look like?

2. What stops you from spending time with God?

3. Do you pray without ceasing? What does that look like for you?

A Time for Justice

*Open your mouth for the mute, for the rights of all
who are destitute. Open your mouth, judge righteously,
defend the rights of the poor and needy.*

Proverbs 31:8–9

O N MAY 30, 2020, two men launched into space. They got into a rocket and left the earth's atmosphere. Five days before this, a man named George Floyd was killed because of his skin color. How have we accomplished so much and yet grown so little?

When I was in graduate school to become a physician assistant, I had to take gross anatomy. That means I cut open dead people. Each of us was assigned in groups of six students to one body for the duration of the class, which meant there were about fifteen cadavers in the room that different groups of students were working on. There were men and women, old and young. There were different skin colors. The first thing we learned was how to remove the skin off of our cadavers. Stay with me here. Once the skin was gone, all the bodies had lungs, hearts, stomachs. There were no signs of their color on the inside. We are all people. When are we going to start acting like it?

I am shielded by the color of my white skin. My heart breaks for the mothers who worry about their sons leaving the house every morning. I can't imagine how I would beg my sons to drive the speed limit, not be in the wrong place, avoid making the wrong eye contact if I were a darker color. I am devastated for the pain that I cannot even understand.

It is time for justice. It is time to weep with those who weep. It is time to stop saying we are color-blind and start acknowledging the disparity between colors. It is time to do better. This is a people problem. This is our problem. We must teach our children the truth. Justice doesn't happen without us fighting for it. We must open our mouths, especially if we are in a place of privilege. Change can occur when we bring our voice to the conversation. But let's not stop there. Seek action. Look for ways to actively combat the destruction of someone's rights. Fight for the rights of the destitute.

Skin color is one issue amid the many inequalities that exist among us. Refugees, women harassed and underpaid in the workplace, human trafficking—the list goes on. It's tempting, when there are so many injustices happening, to become overwhelmed and simply turn away from what we feel we cannot fix. Don't. Face the problems. No, we can't singlehandedly fix them all, but we can use our voices to say it's not OK. It is time for justice.

QUESTIONS

1. Have you ever witnessed or experienced injustice based
    on someone's race, gender or socioeconomic status? If so,
    what did you do?

2. How can you use your voice toward changing
    inequalities?

Conclusion

Where do we go from here? As I said in the introduction, changing our relationship with time requires active participation. There is a difference between passively knowing something is true and actively knowing something is true. When we are passive in our knowledge, we simply allow what we have learned to sit on a shelf deep in the recess of our minds. Maybe sometimes we will reach toward the shelf to reference what we have learned, but the less we employ action, the harder it will be to reach the knowledge. The shelf will always appear just out of reach.

Action is required. We must recognize that what we do with our time matters. We as humans do not exist outside of time. And once we truly understand and embrace the intimacy of our relationship with time, as well as our dependence on time, we begin to see each second, minute and hour as a gift specifically created for us by God.

What will you do with that gift?

Acknowledgements

It takes time to write a book. I would not have been able to complete this endeavor without the unwavering support of Ben. If I haven't referenced it enough in the book, raising young children is hard work, and I could not be both Mom and Author without him.

Mom and Dad, I know any success of this book is thanks to the hundreds of copies you have already committed to purchase. Having received my love of writing equally from both of you, I am so thankful for the permission to dream that you have always encouraged within me.

Dete Meserve, you were an educator and an encourager. Your patience in sharing what you have learned as an author allowed me to press on when I was unsure if I could do this. You are a trailblazer, and I am so thankful.

To my family and friends, who have cheered me on, thank you! When I cried about the fears that come from doing this alone, you heard me. When I imagined what *might* be, you told me it *would* be. You surrounded me with an assurance that this could be done. Thank you!

About the Author

Meredith Barnes has a colorful professional history including in advertising for the Anaheim Angels, and as a costume designer, an orthopedic Physician Assistant, a cycle instructor, a seamstress and a writer. After receiving a Bachelor's of Art degree in Theology from Loyola Marymount University she went on to earn a Master's Degree in Medical Science from Midwestern University.

She is a mother to three energetic and curious boys. She currently resides in Southern California, where she grew up, but considers herself an honorary Midwesterner—both her parents are from the Midwest and she has spent every summer of her life in Michigan. She lived in Chicago for 10 years where she met her husband Ben. Since they moved to California five years ago, he continues to commute back to Chicago for work at least once a month.

Meredith was diagnosed with the autoimmune disease, Juvenile Rheumatoid Arthritis at the age of 8. This significantly molded her childhood experience. Her illness has been a strong motivation for her present day passion for health and wellness.

Meredith doesn't remember a time when she didn't know that God was part of her life. Raised in a liturgical church tradition, after moving to Chicago she joined a large inner city church that did much of its connecting through small groups. It was there that she formed many strong faith friendships with other women. Currently worshiping with a church plant in Pasadena, California she has been involved in steering women's and children's ministries.

While raising her sons takes up most of her days, she still attempts to find time to work on multiple passion projects. Her pleasurable pastimes have included international travel, writing music, and reading (she never goes anywhere without a book in her bag!). She is a blogger on Instagram under the handle "FrecklesandFortitude". She can also be followed at her website: www.frecklesandfortitude.com, where she is committed to finding faith and beauty in her everyday.